D0782416

# THE DEAN OF SHANDONG

I have been a son, a brother, a minister of the emperor, a teacher, a husband, and a father, and I have sons, nephews, and grandchildren. What I have given to my times has been inadequate. Where I have been inadequate is that I have not helped my emperor to unify the empire and bring order to the country. I am truly ashamed to have held all my various offices and ranks without success and wonder how I can repay the gifts of heaven and earth.[1]

—FENG TAO, TENTH-CENTURY
CHINESE BUREAUCRAT

1. Quoted in Wang Gungwu, "Feng Tao: An Essay on Confucian Loyalty," *Confucian Personalities,* ed. Arthur F. Wright and Denis Twitchett (Stanford, Calif.: Stanford University Press, 1962), p. 145.

# The Dean of Shandong

## CONFESSIONS OF A MINOR BUREAUCRAT AT A CHINESE UNIVERSITY

### DANIEL A. BELL

PRINCETON UNIVERSITY PRESS

PRINCETON & OXFORD

Published by Princeton University Press
41 William Street, Princeton, New Jersey 08540
99 Banbury Road, Oxford OX2 6JX

press.princeton.edu

All Rights Reserved

ISBN: 978-0-691-24712-0
ISBN: (e-book): 978-0-691-24713-7

British Library Cataloging-in-Publication Data is available

Editorial: Rob Tempio and Chloe Coy
Production Editorial: Jenny Wolkowicki
Jacket design: Katie Osborne
Production: Erin Suydam
Publicity: Alyssa Sanford and Carmen Jimenez
Copyeditor: Madeleine Adams

Jacket images: Select icons by OpenMoji

This book has been composed in Arno Pro

Printed on acid-free paper. ∞

Printed in the United States of America

10 9 8 7 6 5 4 3 2 1

For My Unicitée

# CONTENTS

# ACKNOWLEDGMENTS

THIS BOOK DRAWS on my experience serving as dean of the School of Political Science and Public Administration at Shandong University from 2017 to 2022. I am most grateful to colleagues and students. I may not have met expectations *qua* dean, but I hope this book will show my appreciation. Shandong University is a uniquely nourishing environment for learning and friendship.

I am particularly grateful to my wonderful editor Rob Tempio, who pushed me to revise and revise until I hit the right note. I would also like to thank three anonymous referees for long and constructive reports and Shadi Bartsch-Zimmer, James Hankins, and my sister Valérie for encouragement and detailed comments on earlier drafts. I am also grateful to Madeleine Adams for excellent copyediting and to Susan Clarke, Chloe Coy, and Jenny Wolkowicki at Princeton University Press for kind and efficient help with the process of publication. This book went through many drafts and I strongly urge those who saw earlier drafts to put them in the dustbin.

I dedicate this book to my wife, Pei. I was separated from family and friends outside mainland China for nearly three years, which was difficult. But Pei and I spent nearly every second together, which not only provided intellectual and emotional nourishment but also helped with my work as dean. I take full responsibility for the many things that went wrong, but to the extent that things went right, much of the credit should go to Pei's informal advice. I would also like to thank our two cats, Zhezhe（喆喆）and Lele（乐乐）, who bring so much joy to our lives, notwithstanding the fact that both Pei and I are allergic to cats.

# Confessions of a Minor Bureaucrat in Shandong Province

I AM NOT NOW nor at any time have ever been a member of the Chinese Communist Party (CCP). Yet I serve as dean of a large faculty of political science in a Chinese university that trains students and provincial cadres to serve the country as Communist Party officials: It's typically a post reserved for members of the CCP, given the political sensitivity of the work. That's part of the surprise. The other part is that I'm a Canadian citizen, born and bred in Montreal, without any Chinese ancestry. On January 1, 2017, I was formally appointed dean of the School of Political Science and Public Administration at Shandong University. I was the first foreign dean of a political science faculty in mainland China's history and it was big news in China. Shandong University is the premier university in a province of more than one hundred million people, and the School of Political Science and Public Administration has more than eighty teachers and more than one thousand students. I was appointed dean not because of a commitment to China's official Marxist ideology but rather because of my scholarly work on Confucianism. Shandong Province is home ground for Confucian culture—both Confucius and Mencius were born in (what is now) Shandong Province and Xunzi taught at the Jixia Academy in central Shandong, the Chinese equivalent of Plato's Academy.[1] Our party secretary, himself a seventy-sixth-generation descendant of Confucius, thought I might be able to help promote Confucianism while internationalizing our faculty and upgrading our academic output.

My appointment as dean is less surprising if it's viewed in the context of the transformation of higher education in China's reform period over the past four decades. There has been a strong push to internationalize China's universities by means such as integrating an international dimension into teaching and research and promoting use of the English language (especially in the sciences, engineering, and business administration). Universities compete to hire foreign-educated faculty and foreign teachers and they provide funding for research stays for Chinese teachers and study abroad programs for students. They cooperate with foreign partners and the government provides support for the establishment of campuses of foreign universities such as New York University in Shanghai. Leading universities such as Tsinghua University in Beijing try to compete with the best universities in the West and they have steadily moved up international academic rankings.[2] Shandong University may have been slow to internationalize but it has tried hard to catch up.[3] Internationalization, however, does not necessarily mean Westernization. Over the past decade, the privileging of Western thought in knowledge production (especially in the humanities and social sciences) has been called into question. Internationalization is increasingly viewed as a two-way street that brings foreign knowledge to China and Chinese knowledge to the world.[4] In that context, it made sense to hire as dean at Shandong University a foreign Confucian-oriented scholar, who could both promote internationalization of the university and help bring China's own traditions to the rest of the world.

As much as I'd like to tell a happy or inspiring story of my time serving as a minor bureaucrat in Shandong Province, it's largely a tale of bungles and misunderstandings. But my post as dean has provided a unique vantage point to learn about Chinese academia and China's political system. This book is an effort to share what I've learned over the past five years serving as dean. It's written in a self-mocking and playful voice, but it's not a memoir. The aim is to share insights, via my experience, about the inner workings of Chinese academia and to draw implications for China's broader political system. The book consists of short, interconnected essays that proceed roughly in chronological order.

First, some background. I need to say something about Confucianism and its revival in China over the past three decades or so. The Confucian tradition has frequently been pronounced dead in China since the early twentieth century, but it has made a dramatic comeback. Then I'll say something about my own background: How did someone from a humble working-class background in Montreal end up as a minor bureaucrat in a relatively conservative Chinese province that's unusually resistant to change?[5] I also need to explain the form of the book. It draws on my personal experience for the purpose of shedding light on Chinese academia and the political system, but why the frequent confessions of things gone wrong? The reader may also wonder: What is my political agenda? I need to come clean. I'll end this introduction with a brief summary of the book.

## The Confucian Comeback

Confucianism is an ethical tradition propagated by Confucius (c. 551–479 BCE). Confucius (*Kongzi* in Chinese) viewed himself as the transmitter of an older tradition that he tried to revitalize in his own day. He was born near present-day Qufu in Shandong Province (today, Qufu is an administrative region with about 650,000 inhabitants, among whom nearly one-fifth share the surname of Kong and trace their family ancestry to Kongzi). Confucius traveled from state to state—China had not yet been unified—aiming to persuade rulers of the need to rule with morality. He failed in his political ambitions and settled for the life of a teacher. His ideas and aphorisms were recorded for posterity by his disciples in the *Analects*. Confucius is often shown in dialogue with his students and he emerges as a wise, compassionate, humble, and even humorous human being. His most influential followers, Mencius (*Mengzi* in Chinese, c. 372–289 BCE) and Xunzi (c. 310–235 BCE), also had less-than-illustrious careers as public officials and settled for teaching careers in (what is now) Shandong Province.

Confucianism was suppressed in the short-lived Qin Dynasty (221–206 BCE) by the self-proclaimed first Emperor of China, Qin Shi Huang. During the Han Dynasty (206 BCE–220 CE), Confucius's thoughts received official sanction and were further developed into a system known as *Rujia* in Chinese (the term "Confucianism" is a Western invention; it is misleading because Confucius was not the founder of a tradition in the sense that, say, Jesus Christ was the founder of Christianity). Confucianism was the mainstream political ideology for much of subsequent imperial Chinese history until the collapse of the imperial system in 1911. The Confucian tradition is immensely diverse and it has been constantly enriched with insights from Daoism, Legalism, and Buddhism, and, more recently, liberalism, democracy, and feminism. But it has certain core commitments. The tradition is based on the assumption that the good life lies in nourishing harmonious social relationships, starting with the family and extending outward. The good life is a never-ending quest to improve oneself by study, rituals, and learning from other people (it's not easy: Confucius said he reached the stage when his desires conformed to what he ought to do at the age of 70, or the equivalent of about 105 years old today). The best life lies in serving the political community with wisdom and humaneness (仁 *ren*). In practice, it typically means striving to be a public official. Only a minority of exemplary persons (君子 *junzi*) can lead the best life because most people are too preoccupied with mundane concerns. The ideal political community is a unified state whose rulers succeed to power on the basis of merit rather than lineage. Public officials should aim to provide basic material well-being for the people by means such as a fair distribution of land and low taxation, and (then) try to improve them morally. They should rule with a light touch: through education, moral example, and rituals, with punishment as a last resort. Such ideas had a profound influence on the value system of public officials in Chinese imperial history; in the Ming and Qing dynasties, officials were selected by means of rigorous examinations that tested for knowledge of the Confucian classics (the Emperor was not selected by examination, but he was often educated in the Confucian classics). Once public officials assumed power, however, political reality often got in the way of humane rule and they often relied on "Legalist" harsh laws aimed at strengthening the state rather than benefiting the people.[6]

The end of imperial rule seemed to signal the end of the Confucian tradition. Intellectuals and political reformers, whatever their political stripe, blamed the tradition for China's "backwardness" (with a few exceptions, such as the "last Confucian," Liang Shuming).[7] From the May 4, 1919, movement onward, the dominant tradition was anti-traditionalism. The victory of the Chinese Communist Party in 1949 seemed to deliver the final blow to Confucianism. Instead of looking backward to such "feudal" traditions as Confucianism, the Chinese people were encouraged to look forward to a bright new communist future. Such anti-traditionalism took an extreme form in the Cultural Revolution, when Red Guards were encouraged to stamp out all remnants of "old society," including ransacking Confucius's grave in Qufu.

Today, it seems that the anti-traditionalists were on the wrong side of history. Chinese intellectuals commonly view themselves as part of a culture with a long history, with Confucianism as its core. Aspects of Marxist-Leninism that took hold in China—the prioritization of poverty alleviation and the need for a politically enlightened "avant-garde" to lead the transition to a morally superior form of social organization—resonated with older Confucian ideas about the need to select and promote public officials with superior ability and virtue who strive for the material and moral well-being of the people. To the extent that China's experiment with communism has anything to offer to future generations, it can be seen as an effort to build on, rather than replace, older traditions. Hence, it should not be surprising that the CCP has moved closer to officially embracing Confucianism. The Confucian classics are being taught at Communist Party schools, the educational curriculum in primary and secondary schools is being modified to teach more Confucianism, and there are more references to Confucian values in speeches and policy documents. The opening ceremony of the 2008 Summer Olympics in Beijing, vetted by the Chinese Politburo, seemed to put an official imprimatur on the Confucianization of the party: Marx and Mao were gone, and Confucius was shown as China's face to the world. Abroad, the government has been promoting Confucianism via branches of the Confucius Institute, a Chinese language and culture center similar to France's Alliance Française and Germany's Goethe Institute. The Confucius Institutes have been controversial in Western countries, but they are often welcomed in other parts of the world and sponsor, for example, workshops that compare the relational view of the self in Confucian and Ubuntu ethics.[8]

But the revival of Confucianism is not just government-sponsored. There has been a resurgence of interest among critical intellectuals in China. Jiang Qing, mainland China's most influential Confucian-inspired political theorist, was first forced to read the Confucian classics in order to denounce them in the Cultural Revolution. The more he read, however, the more he realized that Confucianism was not as bad as advertised and he saved his intellectual curiosity for more propitious times. Today, he runs an independent Confucian Academy in remote Guizhou Province and argues for a political institution composed of Confucian scholars with veto power over policies as well as a symbolic monarch selected from the Kong family descendants.[9] His works, not surprisingly, have been censored in mainland China but that hasn't stopped the explosion of academic research inspired by the Confucian tradition, leading to a kind of reverse brain drain from the United States back to China. Tu Weiming, the most influential exponent of Confucianism in the West, retired from his post at Harvard to lead the Institute of Advanced Humanistic Studies at Peking University. He was followed a few years later by Roger Ames, the celebrated translator and interpreter of the Confucian classics: Ames retired from the University of Hawaii to become the

Humanities Chair Professor at Peking University. The younger Confucian political theorist Bai Tongdong left a tenured job in the United States to become the Dongfang Professor of Philosophy at Fudan University.[10] The cross-cultural psychologist Peng Kaiping, who carried out rigorous experiments showing that Chinese were more likely than Americans to use Confucian-style contextual and dialectical approaches to solving problems,[11] left a tenured post at Berkeley to become dean of Tsinghua's School of Social Sciences. Notwithstanding increased censorship, such scholars are attracted by vibrant academic debates inspired by the Confucian tradition in mainland China. Periodicals such as *Culture, History, and Philosophy* (文史哲) and *Confucius Research* (孔子研究)—both edited by Shandong University's Wang Xuedian[12]—and websites such as *Rujiawang* provide prestigious channels for the dissemination of Confucian academic works. In the twentieth century, academic Confucianism had relocated to Hong Kong, Taiwan, and the United States. Today, the center is shifting once again, back to mainland China.

These political and academic developments are supported by economic factors. China is an economic superpower, and with economic might comes cultural pride (not to mention increased funding for the humanities and higher academic salaries). Max Weber's argument that Confucianism is not conducive to economic development has been widely questioned in view of the economic success of East Asian states with a Confucian heritage. Unlike with Islam, Hinduism, and Buddhism, there has never been an organized Confucian resistance to economic modernization. Quite the opposite: A this-worldly outlook combined with values such as respect for education and concern for future generations may have contributed to economic growth. But modernity also has a downside: It often leads to atomism and psychological anxiety. The competition for social status and material resources becomes fiercer and fiercer, with declining social responsibility and other-regarding outlooks. Communitarian ways of life and civility break down. Even those who make it to the top ask, "What now?" Making money, they realize, doesn't necessarily lead to well-being. It is only a means to the good life, but what exactly is the good life? Is it just about fighting for one's interests? Most people—in China, at least—do not want to be viewed as individualistic. The idea of focusing solely on individual well-being or happiness seems too self-centered. To feel good about ourselves, we also need to be good to others. Here's where Confucianism comes in: The tradition emphasizes that the good life lies in social relationships and commitment to the family, expanding outward. In the Chinese context, Confucian ethics is the obvious resource to help fill the moral vacuum that often accompanies modernization.[13]

In short, this mix of political, academic, economic, and psychological trends helps to explain the revival of Confucianism in China. But I don't want to overstate things. The Confucian comeback seems to have stalled of late. It's not just elderly cadres still influenced by Maoist antipathy to tradition who condemn efforts to promote value systems outside a rigid Marxist framework: As we will see (chapter 7), the Marxist tradition has been making a strong and surprising comeback and communist ideals increasingly set the political priorities and influence academic debates. On the other side of the ideological spectrum, liberal academics in China often look askance at Confucian-inspired defenses of social hierarchy and political meritocracy and blame Confucianism for China's authoritarian tendencies in the family and politics. Not to mention that Confucianism has yet to make a substantial impact among China's minority groups such as Tibetans and Uyghurs. So it's a huge mistake to equate Chinese culture with Confucianism.

That said, Confucianism's greatest impact—in terms of everyday social practices, people's self-identification, as well as political support—is strongest in Shandong Province, the home of the Confucian tradition. The license plates for the province start with the character 鲁 (*Lu*), the name of Confucius's long-defunct small state.[14] Shandong Airlines has quotations from the *Analects of Confucius* above seats on its airplanes.[15] Village leaders in the Shandong countryside teach Confucian classics to young children.[16] The sociologist Anna Sun argues that the modern Chinese state's effort to promote Confucianism began in September 2004, during the celebration of Confucius's 2,555th birthday in Qufu.[17] In imperial China, government officials were in charge of annual ceremonies to commemorate Confucius at the Confucian temple in Qufu, but the rites were discontinued after the collapse of the Qing Dynasty in 1911. In September 2004, for the first time since the founding of the People's Republic, the state officially took over, with government representatives presiding over the rites, and the ceremony is now broadcast on national television. On November 26, 2013, President Xi himself visited Qufu and gave a speech that praised Confucian culture and criticized the destruction of the Cultural Revolution. He visited a Confucian academy and said that he would diligently read two books on the Confucian classics that were handed to him by the academy's director. In 2016, the government officially established the Academy for the Education of Virtuous Public Officials (政德教育学院) in Qufu, which provides education in the Confucian classics for mid-level cadres from the whole country. So it should not come as a big surprise that Shandong University hired a dean of political science and public administration largely on account of his scholarly writings on the contemporary social and political implications of Confucianism, even though the scholar is neither Chinese nor a member of the CCP. But how did I end up as a Confucian scholar in China, the reader may wonder?

## From Communitarianism to Confucianism

Like the early Confucians, I settled on the life of a teacher as a second choice. As a boy, I dreamed of being a professional hockey player for the Montreal Canadiens. But the hockey world was too competitive, so I went to Oxford to study political theory. I'm from a mixed Jewish and Catholic background and I had no prior interest in China, nor did I study Chinese philosophy at Oxford. So why go to China? It's not just me who needs to answer this sort of question. "Why did you come to China?" is the most common question asked of any foreigner living in China. In my case, I'd answer with a joke: Do you want the rational story or the true story? Of course, people want to hear the true story. Here it is. At Oxford, I fell in love with a fellow graduate student from China. We married shortly thereafter, and then I learned the language and became fascinated by Chinese culture. Since our divorce in 2020, however, I tell the rational story. Here it is. My doctoral thesis at Oxford was an attempt to present and defend contemporary "Western" communitarian theory against its liberal critics. Communitarianism is the idea that human identities are largely shaped by different kinds of constitutive communities (or social relations) and that this conception of human nature should inform our moral and political judgments as well as policies and institutions. We live most of our lives in social groups, like lions who live in prides rather than individualistic tigers who live alone most of the time. Those communities shape, and ought to shape, our moral and political judgments, and we have a strong obligation to support and nourish the particular communities that provide meaning for our lives, without which we'd be disoriented, deeply lonely, and incapable of informed moral and political judgment.[18]

I moved to Singapore for my first academic job, and my colleagues tended to argue about "Asian values." Although I wasn't persuaded of the utility of such a nebulous term, I became interested when the debate focused on Confucian values. I learned that Confucianism has a lot in common with communitarian themes such as the relational idea of the self and the importance of culture and history for moral and political reasoning, but I came to view Confucianism as a deeper and richer tradition, with thousands of years of history, unlike communitarianism, which is a more recent offshoot of liberalism. Plus, some themes in the Confucian tradition—filial piety, the importance of ritual, diversity in harmony, and political meritocracy—are absent from communitarian debates and worth exploring in academic works. So I shifted my research interests to Confucianism. And with the revival of the Confucian tradition in China, it made sense to move to China to learn about those debates. Eventually, I ended up in Shandong Province, the home of Confucian culture.

"When do you plan to go home?" is the second most common question asked of foreigners living in China. There is an assumption that we will not stay here forever because of the different culture and the supposedly "evil" political system, not to mention that life is usually more comfortable in wealthier, pollution-free, and less crowded Western countries. People no longer ask me that question. There is an assumption, which will probably turn out to be correct, that I will stay here forever, or, to be more precise, until I die. The first reason, known to my friends, is that I recently married a younger scholar deeply steeped in Chinese culture who plans to develop her career in Chinese academia. The second reason is that I've become a minor bureaucrat in the Chinese political system: Since January 2017, I've been dean of the School of Political Science and Public Administration at Shandong University. This kind of job wouldn't be offered to an academic tourist, and there's an assumption that I will stay in my adopted homeland for the rest of my days. I've been offered a difficult-to-obtain Chinese "green card" (永久居留证), which grants permanent residency in China, and I've stayed here throughout the Covid crisis. The next step, which I may try to realize one day, is to apply for Chinese citizenship.

## A Political Agenda?

The reader may be left with lingering doubts about my political agenda. I may not be a Communist Party member, but I'm still a servant of the Chinese state. Does it follow that I won't criticize that state or that I've become an apologist for the political system? Let me try to respond. I do have an agenda and I should come clean about normative commitments. I worry about the demonization of China and especially of its political system. I think much thinking and policy making in Western countries is based on crude stereotypes about China's political system, such as the view that the CCP exercises total control over intellectual discourse and there is no room for independent thinking. The reality is much more complex, as I hope to show.

I most certainly do not want to deny that increased demonization is related to worrisome developments in Chinese politics over the past decade or so. The CCP—to a certain extent—has become more repressive at home and more aggressive abroad. The end of presidential term limits for China's top leader leaves open the possibility of a return to Maoist-style personal dictatorship. Increased censorship demoralizes academics, journalists, and artists. The mass incarceration of Uyghurs in Xinjiang seems like a gross overreaction to the threat of terrorism and religious extremism. Hong Kong's National Security Law has seriously eroded the rule of law and freedom of speech in the territory, if not the one country, two systems model as a whole. China's refusal to condemn Russia's invasion of Ukraine makes a mockery of its commitment to respect for territorial boundaries and state sovereignty. When I look at some of the things I wrote in the past, I realize that I was much too naïve in thinking that China would move toward a more humane political system, informed first and foremost by Confucian values and with more tolerance for social and political dissent. That might happen someday in the future, but it looks as though we will have to wait a long time, just as Confucius had to wait five centuries to see his political ideals (partly) realized in the Han Dynasty. Not to mention that the Legalist tradition and its modern Leninist incarnation, with its totalitarian-like aspirations to control every aspect of society by means of fear and harsh punishment, often informs the decisions of political leaders, especially in times of social crisis.

Still, I think the demonization of the CCP needs to be countered. For one thing, the demonization reinforces repressive trends in China and benefits security-obsessed hard-liners in China's political system.[19] China's leaders are not about to take serious political risks and promote democratic experimentation when they feel that the whole political establishment of the world's most powerful country seems united in its fight against them.[20] Chinese leaders may be paranoid, but their paranoia is well-founded.[21] So both sides are locked in a vicious political cycle, with the United States and its Western allies growing more antagonistic and warlike, and China reinforcing its walls and repressing alternative political voices. Second, it's worth asking if the worrisome political developments in China of the past few years really do threaten the West. China has neither the intention nor the ability to export its political system abroad. And how can China pose a greater existential threat to the United States than the former Soviet Union, which threatened to annihilate the United States in a nuclear war? China hasn't gone to war with anybody since 1979, and even the most hawkish voices in the Chinese military establishment do not threaten war against the United States.[22] The idea that China would seek to go to war against the United States anywhere near its territory is crazy (on the other hand, China is surrounded by U.S. military bases, and it's not absurd for Chinese policy makers to worry that the United States and its allies might launch a war against China).[23] Still, the "China threat" is used as an excuse by the Pentagon for huge new budgets, even as the United States has ended real wars in Iraq and Afghanistan.[24]

It's also worth asking why the CCP has so much support at home if it's as evil as advertised.[25] Cynics will say that it's because the Chinese people are brainwashed by media propaganda and an educational system that praises the government and stifles critical thinking. But that can't be the whole, or even the main, story. Similar views are held by sophisticated intellectuals in China who have good knowledge of alternative viewpoints, not to mention the hundreds of thousands of Chinese students in the United States and the 130 million Chinese tourists who went abroad every year before the pandemic. The main reason for support is that the CCP has presided over the most spectacular economic growth story in global history, with more than eight hundred million people lifted out of poverty. The spread of literacy and university education under the CCP, not to mention extended life expectancy, is an extraordinary achievement. More recent developments have only reinforced growing support for the political system. The anti-corruption drive, however imperfect, has proven hugely popular with ordinary citizens burning with anger at public officials who thrived on bribery and special benefits for themselves. After the initial debacle in Wuhan, the central government largely brought Covid under control. People in China had two years of relative freedom to lead their lives without constraints experienced in the rest of the world, though the highly contagious Omicron variant casts doubt on old methods.[26] The anti-pollution measures that led to blue skies in Beijing and other cities make people happier. Again, there are tons of problems, and things can take a turn for the worse in the future, but a more balanced picture of the CCP is necessary to counter demonization of China's political system.

It's worth keeping in mind that the ninety-six-million-strong CCP includes tens of millions of farmers, workers, entrepreneurs, and intellectuals who have nothing to do with high-level policy making in Beijing. As one might expect of any large organization, some members of the CCP are good people, some are bad, with most in between. In my own experience, most CCP members are talented, hard-working, and sincerely committed to improving the lives of Chinese citizens. Many of my dearest friends are members of the CCP. As far as I'm concerned, demonization of the CCP is patently absurd. I'm employed as dean at a large Chinese university, and most of the senior scholars and administrators are members of the CCP who work hard for the good of our students and teachers. "Evil" is the last word I'd use to describe my friends and colleagues.

So, yes, I do have a political agenda. I aim to de-demonize China's political system. I hope that readers can temporarily set aside preconceptions and judgments about "the" Chinese Communist Party. As a minor bureaucrat in the university system where most leaders are members of the CCP, I see a bafflingly complex organization composed mainly of extremely hard-working public officials with a mixture of motives and diverse perspectives, who argue endlessly about how to put out fires and, when time allows, plan for the long-term good. In this book, I embed my experience as a minor bureaucrat in the broader political system and try to draw implications for that system. Admittedly, my sample size is small and university-based but it comes from prolonged exposure. I try to shed light on a world that is both very important and very hard to understand. I do my best to be truthful. I write about what works and what doesn't. I share my experience in a frank, if not reckless, way, with gentle criticism of others and fierce self-criticism. These stories try to humanize China's political system: to show how things are experienced at the local level, warts and all.[27] I'm a critic of the CCP, but I also see positive things to build on and I do not favor overthrowing the whole system.

## A Note on the Form

This book draws on my personal experience for the purpose of shedding light on Chinese academia and the political system, but why the frequent confessions of things gone wrong? My academic excuse is that I've tried writing books in other forms—my first two books were in dialogue form, then I wrote conventional academic books, then a book of short essays, then a book (with Avner de-Shalit) that mixes personal experience with theorizing about different cities, then more books in standard academic form (including one co-authored with Wang Pei)—and I needed a new intellectual challenge. The truth is that it's some mixture of Jewish guilt, Catholic sin, and Confucian shame, and I'd need years of therapy to make sense of the muck. That said, it's worth distinguishing between two types of confessional books. One type is to confess for the sake of exposing errors from the perspective of a newly discovered moral truth. Augustine's *Confessions* is written in that vein (he found God) and so is *From Emperor to Citizen*, the autobiography of China's last Emperor, Pu Yi (he found Communism).[28] The second type is to confess errors for the sake of truth, and to express regret that a simpler life with fewer desires and less ambition might have led to fewer errors. It's not a story of moral progress and may be a story of moral regress. Rousseau's *Confessions* is the first and still the best book written in that genre. My book is of the second type. I try to follow Rousseau's self-mocking tone, though without the self-pity. In contrast with Rousseau, however, my book is *not* a memoir: The truth I seek is not self-understanding but understanding of China. I invoke my personal experience only if it sheds light on social and political life in contemporary China, with its contradictions, diversity, and charm. Confessional frankness is meant to generate understanding and sympathy not for myself, but for other people I encountered during my misadventures.

## Outline of the Book

It's best to read this short book in chronological order and it can be read in one sitting. It's written with a light touch but I'll try to make it intellectually worthwhile. For the really busy readers out there, the summary will help you to choose parts of the book that seem to be of greater interest.

1. **Dye and Dynamism.** I show why hair color matters so much for public officials in the Chinese political system, from the very top leaders in Beijing to university administrators in remote provinces. It sounds silly, but it's not.

2. **The Harmony Secretary.** I discuss the role of the party secretary in the university system. Although I'm not crazy about what they do *qua* ideological overseers, I admire their work helping to maintain and promote social harmony in the university.

3. **On Collective Leadership.** I evaluate the advantages and disadvantages of collective leadership in contemporary Chinese politics and show how we have similar mechanisms at the faculty level at Shandong University.

4. **What's Wrong with Corruption?** I recount my experience of being caught up in the early days of modern China's most systematic anti-corruption campaign. Counterintuitively, perhaps, I'm rooting for a bit more tolerance of potentially corrupt behavior.

5. **Drinking without Limits.** I discuss Shandong's drinking culture and how it affects my work as dean. Meals with teachers and students are almost always fortified with endless toasts, yet few people drive drunk. This essay explains why, drawing on my own unhappy experience.

6. **Teaching Confucianism in China.** I describe the challenges of teaching Confucianism (in English) to foreign students and (in Chinese) to Chinese students in China. It requires different strategies beyond bookish learning.

7. **The Communist Comeback.** In 2008, I pronounced that Marxism was dead in China. To my surprise, it has made a dramatic comeback and I show its impact on university life. I argue that China's political future is likely to be shaped by both Confucianism and Communism.

8. **Censorship, Formal and Informal.** I discuss my experience with censorship in China. Not surprisingly, the heavy hand of the state constrains what can be published in China, but I try to show that informal constraints in the West also curtail what can be published about Chinese politics in mainstream media outlets.

9. **Academic Meritocracy, Chinese-Style.** Notwithstanding increased censorship and political constraints, there is intense competition among Chinese universities to improve academically. I show how our faculty has been mobilized to that effect, with some unintended consequences, such as penalizing Chinese academics who do not write well in English.

10. **A Critique of Cuteness.** I discuss the political relevance of the culture of cuteness in China. "Playing cute" can have politically disastrous consequences, and it helps to explain my own failures as a minor bureaucrat.

11. **The Case for Symbolic Leadership.** I draw on my own experience as a symbolic leader at the end of my term as dean to argue that symbolic monarchy is appropriate for modern societies.

# 1

# Dye and Dynamism

FORMER PRESIDENT HU JINTAO is perhaps the most boring leader in modern times. His only recorded joke came when he was visiting the United States in 2007. The then-governor of New Jersey, James McGreevey, told Hu—whose hair was jet-black—that he did not look his fifty-nine years. Hu replied: "China would be happy to share its technology in this area."[1] The use of hair dye for political leaders has a long history in China. Why do Chinese leaders dye their hair? It has nothing to do with communist ideology. The roots go way back in Chinese history. In the Eastern Jin Dynasty (317–420), the medical scientist Ge Hong recorded a secret recipe for dyeing hair black in the palace.[2] Even today, it's not easy: A professional coiffeur estimates that Chinese politicians need to touch up their hair roots every ten days or so to maintain that jet-black look.[3] Why bother dyeing one's hair? The basic idea is that black-haired rulers project an image of vigor and energy: They work hard for the good of the people.

Conversely, as Mencius put it in the fourth century BCE, "white-haired people" should be cared for rather than engage in heavy work (IA.7). It would be strange, in a Chinese context, to be ruled by "white-haired people." As the hair stylist

Hong Haiting put it, "I don't want to see my leader with grey hair. It will make him look old . . . like he's about to die! How could a person like that lead our country? This is a political issue, not a lifestyle one."[4] White hair is a sign that one has left politics, either by force or voluntarily. In the first camp, former Politburo member Zhou Yongkang became the highest-ranking victim of President Xi's anti-corruption campaign. When he appeared in court, his jet-black hair had turned completely white. In the second camp, retired former premier Zhu Rongji has gone naturally white.[5] The former president Jiang Zemin continued to dye his hair for public appearances well into his nineties, a sign that he still exercised some power behind the scenes.

Of course, more contemporary factors are also at play. The collective leadership system in China, developed after a horrible experience with Chairman Mao's arbitrary one-man rule that culminated in the Cultural Revolution, deemphasizes individuality. Policy making is supposed to be the product of collective deliberation among members of the Standing Committee of the Politburo, and individual leaders are not supposed to stick out too much. Here, Hu Jintao was a master. His jet-black hair blended with other leaders who dyed their hair in an identical way, sending the message that he really was an equal among the (eight) other members of the Standing Committee.

The collective leadership system under President Hu had a major drawback, however. Each top leader was an equal, in charge of a policy area, and each leader had de facto veto power over decisions that affected his constituency's interests. It was impossible to tackle vested interests that blocked necessary reform.[6] Tackling corruption, for example, required making lots of enemies, and neither President Hu nor other members of the Standing Committee of the Politburo had the power (or perhaps the courage) to do so. In came President Xi in 2012. The

Standing Committee was reduced from nine to seven members, Xi took charge of newly established leading groups in charge of reform, and six years later Chinese lawmakers approved changes to the constitution abolishing presidential term limits, effectively allowing President Xi to rule longer than the two five-year terms that had limited Presidents Jiang and Hu. President Xi emerged, as the political scientist Wang Shaoguang put it, as the first among equals. On the plus side, he has the power to tackle vested interests: President Xi carried out the longest and most sustained anti-corruption drive in CCP history and took on economic interests that blocked measures to clean up the environment and redistribute wealth from the rich to the poor. On the negative side, there are fewer checks on bad decision-making and growing constraints on freedom of speech, and the lack of a clear successor contributes to worries about the long-term stability of the political system.

In 2019, President Xi broke another long-standing political norm: He appeared in public with streaks of gray in his hair.[7] The topic was off limits for the domestic media, but the Western media speculated that President Xi meant to affirm his superior power relative to other members of the Standing Committee of the Politburo. Hung Huang, a media personality who grew up among political elites in Beijing the 1960s and 1970s, remarks that leaders have traditionally dyed their hair black as a kind of "conformity to a single regimented style as a sign of unison and agreement. . . . It's one that Xi—who now clearly stands above everyone else—no longer needs."[8] Does President Xi's more "natural" appearance reflect the end of collective leadership?[9] It's too early to tell. What I can predict is that even if Xi proves to be a Putin-like ruler who rules for decades with largely unchecked power, he will not let his hair turn completely white. The belief that white-haired people are not supposed to rule is perhaps the one article in China's unwritten constitution that cannot be violated.

Political norms that influence the highest echelons of Chinese politics often filter down to lower levels of the bureaucracy. I'm dean of a large faculty at Shandong University—with more than one thousand students and eighty professors—and our decisions need to be approved by a group of leaders, including four vice-deans and three party secretaries, that we half-jokingly refer to as a system of collective leadership. Each leader is in charge of a different aspect of the faculty and decisions need to be discussed with other leaders at bi-weekly meetings, to be approved (or rejected) following extensive deliberation.[10] At meetings, we all bring our notebooks and assiduously take notes, especially when the leaders speak.[11] Like Xi et al., our attire is neither too formal nor too casual, meant to suggest a commitment to work and closeness to the people. Not surprisingly, we are also constrained by the black-hair norm. Those of us with white hair need to dye our hair black to project an image of energy and vigor in our efforts to serve the university. In my case, it would look strange if I dyed my hair black, so I dye it brown, the more natural-looking color given my white skin pigmentation.

## It's the Hair, Stupid

I confess, however, that my hair dyeing has earlier roots. It all started when I was thirty-nine years old, living in Hong Kong and teaching at the City University of Hong Kong. My university president told visiting guests that I was in my forties. My badminton partner—a remarkably fit graduate student—said that I looked like a distinguished professor. I took that as code for "old professor," a thought triggered by my rapidly graying hair (or perhaps he was gently saying that I should bow out to make room for a successor on the badminton court). I wasn't too happy, but I realized that I had to face the reality that I looked older than my age. My father and grandfather went gray in their thirties, and I was continuing the family tradition.

My Chinese mother-in-law had other ideas. She had been living with us for about ten years, and I loved her (and still love her) very much. My Chinese friends praised my commitment to filial piety, but in fact she took care of us. She helped in our moment of greatest need—when our son Julien was born. She cooked and cleaned, with never a complaint. She had served in the Korean War—where she met and married her husband, a fellow soldier in the People's Liberation Army—and was used to hardship. But she wasn't a blind follower of party doctrine. She recalled that some landlords executed in the early 1950s were good people who cared for their employees. And she had a sly sense of humor; we'd sometimes smile at one another when her deadly earnest husband blindly defended party rule. Unlike the stereotypical mother-in-law in the West, she did not try to impose her demanding standards on me or try to make me feel guilty for not living up to those standards. She knew I was from a different culture and tolerated variations of ways of life within the family. With one exception: She could not stand my white hair. I was the first foreigner she had seen close up and she thought I instantiated the form of Western beauty (she would criticize Hollywood movie stars for deviating from the standard of beauty I had set; I confess that I never tried to correct her). So my mother-in-law was deeply disappointed when my hair began to turn gray and she pressured me to dye my hair. I told her that male academics don't dye their hair, but she didn't care. Even in the Cultural Revolution, she said, we—men and women—dyed our hair![12]

After two or three years of her nagging, I succumbed. I had been offered a one-year fellowship at Stanford's Center for Advanced Study in the Behavioral Sciences in 2003–2004 and I thought it would be a good opportunity to start a new look without being embarrassed in front of my colleagues and students. Supervised by my mother-in-law, our Filipina domestic helper dyed my hair brown the day before I left for California. I worried about the doorman's reaction, so I wore a baseball cap as I stepped out of our university housing complex. On the plane, fortified by a couple of drinks, I could finally relax. I took a good look in the toilet's mirror, and I confess that I was pleased by the result. I was transformed into a younger man and nobody would know it![13]

Of course, the process of decay did not take long. A few weeks later, streaks of gray hair started showing on my temples and sideburns, and it was affecting my mood. My family had stayed in Hong Kong, so I flew back to Hong Kong for a break. My mother-in-law was not happy with what she saw. So we did another hair job, with a lighter color. I did venture to my university and one younger female colleague, who had previously shown no interest, said I looked "thinner." I took that as code for "more handsome."

When I returned to Palo Alto, I thought my fellow fellows wouldn't notice the change, but Elaine Scarry—author of *On Beauty and Being Just*—said that she liked my new hair color. Scarry's book—perhaps the most beautifully written work in contemporary Anglophone political theory—argues that a concern for beauty inspires a concern for justice.[14] So, I took her compliment as some sort of allusion to moral progress. Not only that. The more I thought about it, the more it seemed unjust that it was okay for women to dye their hair but not for men to do so. Surely it was a legacy of the patriarchal age, when women were viewed as sex objects made for men's pleasure? If men dye their hair, it's a way of breaking down those patriarchal norms. We should also be judged by our appearances; it's not just the prerogative of oppressed women! Downgrading men is a way of upgrading women. The day when men are viewed as just as vain as women, it will break down the stereotype that men are more rational, and both sexes can be viewed as equals in other spheres of social life.[15]

I kept the feminist case for dyeing men's hair to myself, but I still think it's not a bad argument. A few weeks later, reality again set in. This time, I ventured to a hair stylist in San Jose (about twenty miles from Palo Alto), to make sure I wouldn't run into anyone I knew. The hair stylist asked if I was a politician (perhaps he recalled Ronald Reagan's hair job). I answered, Not yet, but perhaps later. When my fellowship at Stanford expired, our family moved to Beijing, to start a new life there. I was relieved when I noticed that so many men (including academics) dyed their hair in mainland China.[16] For the first time in a long time, I felt at home.

## A Different Life?

Jean-Jacques Rousseau opens *The Confessions* with the famous line, "I have resolved on an enterprise which has no precedent, and which, once complete, will have no imitator. My purpose is to display to my kind a portrait in every way true to nature, and the man I shall portray will be myself."[17] More than 250 years later, Rousseau's *Confessions* remains the most strikingly original book in the genre. But it's a book, one senses, that he would rather not have written. It's a painful read, consisting of relentless self-flagellation and resentment against enemies real and imagined who took advantage of his success and made his life miserable. At the end of Book One, he writes that he could have led a different, much happier life as a good craftsman. It's worth quoting the passage at length:

> Before I abandon myself to my fatal destiny, let me turn for a moment to the prospect that would normally have awaited me had I fallen into the hands of a better master. Nothing suited my character better, nor was more likely to make me happy than the calm and obscure life of a good craftsman, particularly in a superior trade like that of an engraver at Geneva. The work, which was lucrative enough to lead to fortune, would have limited my ambition till the end of my days and have left me honest leisure wherein to cultivate simple tastes. It would have kept me in my sphere, and offered me no means of escaping from it. . . . I should have passed a calm and peaceful life in the security of my faith, in my own country, among my family and friends. That was what my peculiar character required, a life spent in the uniform pursuit of a trade I had chosen, and in a society after my own heart. I should have been a good Christian, a good citizen, a good father, a good friend, a good workman, a good man in every way. I should have been happy in my condition, and should perhaps have been respected. Then, after a life—simple and obscure, but also mild and uneventful—I should have died peacefully in the bosom of my family. Soon, no doubt, I should have been forgotten, but at least I should have been mourned for as long as I was remembered.
>
> But instead . . . what a picture I have to paint! But do not let us anticipate the miseries of my life. I shall have only too much to say to my readers on that melancholy subject.[18]

In my case, I was never very good with my hands, so I could not have been a good craftsman. But I share Rousseau's regrets.

I could have remained an obscure academic with a contented family life. I could have been good to my family, good to my students, and good to my colleagues. Instead, I dyed my hair, which made me more attractive to the ladies and fed my desire for a political role in China. Had I been content with a (not so full) head of gray hair, I would not have lasted so long in China. I would not have had episodes that led to the end of my marriage. I would not have been offered the post of minor bureaucrat in Shandong Province. I would not have become disillusioned about politics. And I would not be writing this book.

# 2

# The Harmony Secretary

WHEN I MEET public officials in China, I'm often asked, why is our image so bad in the West? They say: Of course we have many problems. We're still a relatively poor country in terms of GDP per capita. There's a big gap between rich and poor, pollution is bad, corruption is a problem, and everybody knows about restlessness in Hong Kong and Xinjiang. Perhaps we've overreacted at times and local officials often abuse their power. But we've made some progress, especially in terms of poverty alleviation and combatting corruption. We did a good job of dealing with Covid after the initial debacle in Wuhan (and until the debacle in Shanghai). Unlike other large countries, we haven't gone to war since 1979. We know that we need peace to develop into a humane country. Why can't the West see both sides of the story? How can we pose an existential threat to the West? They have their own history, culture, and political system, and we have neither the desire nor the ability to challenge their way of life. Why can't they leave us alone, let us develop peacefully, and we can work together on dealing with global challenges such as pandemics and climate change?

If I have time, I try to explain that "we" Chinese must do a better job of reducing the gap between what we say and what we do. We should rely more on humane soft power than repression and fear to get things done. I also explain that the West has a strong missionary impulse, dating from the earliest days of Christianity, to export the "truth" about morality and politics abroad. Today, democratic fundamentalism has replaced religious fundamentalism. Westerners tend to think that "good" democratic countries use electoral democracy in the form of one person, one vote to select political leaders and all the rest are "authoritarian" countries that lack political legitimacy. As President Biden put it, there are two types of political systems: democracies with values and autocracies with "lack of values."[1]

Such political dogmatism is a relatively new, post–World War II phenomenon, reinforced by the global reach of U.S. power. In the nineteenth century, liberals such as John Stuart Mill could question the value of one person, one vote and propose alternatives such as extra votes for educated citizens. But today, such views are seen as beyond the moral pale. Electoral democracy is the "end of history," which sets the normative standard for China's political development. Once China modernized economically, it was supposed to become a Western-style liberal democracy, like Japan and South Korea. But now Westerners have lost that hope. They look at the fact that the same political party has been in power for more than seventy years, and they think that there's been no political reform. We—in China—know that's ridiculous. The system here is totally different from, say, the family-run personality cult in North Korea, military dictatorships in Myanmar and Egypt, or absolute monarchies in Saudi Arabia and Brunei. The main difference, we know, is that there has been an effort to reestablish a complex bureaucratic system informed by the ideal of political meritocracy—that is, a political system that aims to select and promote public officials with superior ability and virtue. It's an ongoing project with a large gap between the ideal and reality, and sometimes it's two steps forward and one step backward (or two steps backward and one step forward), but that's what makes our political system distinctive.

Unfortunately, Westerners don't see things that way because they have the view that only the adoption of electoral democracy counts as "real" political reform; the rest is all fake. Worse, if China's political model proves to be successful—if it better provides for the needs of its citizens and impresses other developing countries—Westerners worry that the democratic political model will retreat, if not implode. When Westerners think of political alternatives to electoral democracy, they think of fascism (even though Hitler gained power by means of elections) and Stalin's communism. They think China's political system is fundamentally similar to these evil totalitarian regimes; hence, it needs to be defeated, by war if necessary. That's why some say China poses an existential challenge to the West.

I usually don't have time for such lectures about why the West is having a hard time with China, so I begin with a translation problem. China's key political concepts are often mistranslated into English, which contributes to China's image problem. Terms that sound positive in Chinese can sound negative in English if they are not translated properly. One obvious example is the Chinese character *he* (和), usually (mis)translated as harmony. *He* is a key concept in Confucian ethics and the character was highlighted at the opening ceremony of the 2008 Olympics in Beijing as representing the core of Chinese culture. I remember watching the ceremony on American television and an announcer marveled at the discipline and order displayed by the "harmonious" soldiers at the ceremony, who all seemed to act in complete unison. But I realized that "harmony" gives the wrong impression in English, because it sounds like uniformity and conformity. A harmonious society is one where everybody acts and thinks alike. But that's almost the opposite of what is meant by *he*. Every Chinese intellectual knows the famous saying in the *Analects of Confucius* that exemplary persons value harmony (*he*) but not sameness/uniformity/conformity (君子和而不同 *junzi he er bu tong*).

The contrast between *he* and conformity (*tong*) owes its origin to the *Zuo Zhuan*, where it emerges in the context of a discussion of the idea that the ruler should be open to different political views among advisers. Contemporary social critics have often drawn on the phrase to urge the government to be tolerant of different views and not simply enforce one dominant state ideology on the whole population. To try to stamp out critical views is a recipe for disaster. In other words, the idea of *he* values, if not celebrates, diversity and pluralism. Respect for diversity should take place in a peaceful political order, where the different parts interact and enrich each other through mutual learning. So a better translation of *he* might be "diversity in harmony." At the very least, it's important to explain that the Chinese use of "harmony" respects diversity as opposed to valuing sameness. The musical idea of harmony, with different notes interacting to producing something more beautiful than the sum of the parts, is closer to the Chinese meaning of *he*.

More surprising, perhaps, the Chinese political organs in charge of promoting a better image of the government at home and abroad often undermine their own goals with their mistranslations. Consider the *Xuanchuanbu* (宣传部), not just in charge of censorship but also with authority over Chinese media organs abroad and institutes such as the Confucius Institutes that are supposed to promote Chinese language and culture abroad. Speaking as an academic, I don't like the way they exercise censorship over what we publish in China; it's absurd to put those who do not understand the intricacies of academic argumentation in charge of what academics can say in the public domain. But I recognize that the *Xuanchuanbu* does some valuable work at home in communicating the government's policies, such as how to combat pandemics in an effective way. In principle, there's nothing wrong with promoting Chinese ideas abroad so that foreigners can better understand, if not appreciate, what's going on in China. But the *Xuanchuanbu* undercuts its own mission by mistranslations. For many years, it was officially known as the Propaganda Department, with Orwellian overtones of a totalitarian government trying to pull the wool over its own people's eyes. A few years ago, the *Xuanchuanbu* changed its official translation to "Publicity Department," which is scarcely an improvement. In English, it's okay for private companies to do publicity to sell their products, but a government is supposed to be more neutral. So why not use more neutral terms such as "Communication" or "Public Engagement"? It won't guarantee effective communication of the government's message, but it opens the possibility of success.

Another example is the *Tongyi Zhanxian* (统一战线), officially translated as the "United Front." Far from promoting adherence to the official ideology, the United Front is supposed to provide a voice and political platform for non-communist political parties via institutions such as the Chinese People's Political Consultative Conference (CPPCC). In the CPPCC, non-communist political parties such as the Democratic League deliberate at length about proposals meant to improve society. The United Front is also supposed to help promote Chinese culture and identity among people with Chinese heritage at home and abroad: For example, it sponsors visits by students from Hong Kong to learn about Shandong Province's rich and diverse Chinese culture. My own university has a doctoral program in United Front work, with the aim of teaching students China's political system (including the non-communist elements) and deepening their knowledge about Chinese culture, so that graduates can promote knowledge of and attachment to Chinese culture at home and abroad. But our students do not always learn enough about the Chinese culture they are supposed to promote. And the means employed—long, boring lectures—are often counterproductive. United Front officials have asked for my advice. I say that the best way to promote interest in Chinese culture is to make students learn about the "hundred schools of thought" that flourished in the Spring and Autumn and Warring States periods of ancient China. Many of these fascinating debates about society and politics, such as debates between Confucians and Mohists and between Confucians and Legalists, took place here in (what we now call) Shandong Province. The Jixia Academy (稷下学宫) hosted talks and debates by Mencius, Mozi, and Xunzi, among other luminaries who set the terms of political debate in subsequent Chinese history. Why not rebuild the Jixia Academy, invite contemporary scholars for talks and debates, with students from Hong Kong and elsewhere to witness and participate in these debates?[2] Surely that's a good way to promote pride in Chinese culture. My interlocutors from the United Front say they like the idea, though it has yet to be implemented.

But my point here is about (mis)translation. "United Front" is a literal translation of *Tongyi Zhanxian*, but it sends the wrong message about what the department is supposed to do. The term comes from wartime—when the Chinese Communist Party urged a united front in the form of an alliance with the Kuomintang (KMT, the Chinese Nationalist Party) against Japanese imperialists—and still today it conjures up images of some sort of secretive mission to promote communism in a deadly battle against external enemies. No wonder the work of the United Front sounds so sinister when it's reported abroad.[3] Some of what it does may indeed be problematic—if it involves deceitful influence operations designed to make foreign organizations toe the CCP's line[4]—but much of its work is a useful corrective to, say, an educational system in Hong Kong still heavily influenced by a colonial heritage that promotes hatred for the Chinese political system, if not for Chinese culture as a whole. But how can Westerners see the good side of the United Front if it sounds like an organization from the wartime era that aims to clearly distinguish between friends and enemies so as to defeat the latter? Why not change the name to something like the "Department of Cultural and Political Outreach"? Such terminology better captures the work of the United Front and, unlike the current translation, it does not automatically conjure the image (in English) of political work that's beyond the moral pale in times of peace.

Here's another example of a translation that sends the wrong message to the Anglophone world: the *dangwei shuji* (党委书记), commonly translated as the "party secretary" (or sometimes as the "party chief" or "party boss"). It sounds as though party secretaries have the task of devising and implementing the decisions of the ruling CCP. That's certainly true at the highest levels of government. President Xi Jinping is the "General Secretary" (总书记 *zong shuji*), meaning the number one among the party secretaries. In provinces and cities, the party secretary is the most powerful person in the administrative hierarchy, who does indeed have the task of formulating and executing policies set by the CCP. But it's a different story in companies (public and private), hospitals, and universities, where the *shuji*'s work is not always, or even usually, so political.

I was persuaded to serve as dean at Shandong University by K. *shuji*, the *shuji* of the Qingdao branch of Shandong University. It was a long process. More than ten years ago, K. *shuji* brought me to the campus and asked if I would be willing to serve as dean of the School of Political Science and Public Administration. I tried to suppress a laugh. I expected that we'd be in Qingdao. But we were sixty kilometers away, in the middle of the countryside. The "campus" was an empty field leading to the ocean, with beautiful Lao Shan (a famous Daoist mountain) in the background. He explained that the university would start building the new campus the following year and it should be ready in five years or so. I said, Okay, let's talk again in a few years' time.

Three years later (in 2015), most of the buildings seemed to be more or less in shape. Not only that. There were two majestic buildings: a twelve-story library, the largest (in terms of space) in Asia, and a museum housing archeological treasures from Shandong Province, with illuminated bands at night that mimicked bamboo strips with ancient Chinese characters. The academic buildings had sleek red tile roofs, similar to the German colonial buildings in Qingdao city.[5] The buildings, though distinctive, have Art Deco facades, with large, Beijing-style courtyards in the middle. I asked K. *shuji* if he was worried about climate change: Will this campus be flooded in fifty years' time? He said, No worries; we built it six meters above sea level for that reason. Then he pointed to the building closest to the library and said that half of the building would house "my" faculty and the law faculty would occupy the other half. I was impressed: Only in China, I thought, could a university campus arise from nowhere so quickly.

What about the students? I asked. K. *shuji* said that the campus would open in mid-2017, with more than ten thousand students in six faculties, including mine. In terms of quality, our students are second to none: It's more difficult for a student from Shandong Province to be admitted to Shandong University than for a student from Beijing to be admitted to Tsinghua University.[6] I hadn't yet said yes, but he could tell that I was tempted. He then told me that each student on campus would be required to study the *Analects of Confucius*. K. *shuji* was obviously proud of the Confucian tradition of his ancestors.[7] Then he took me out to lunch: an oceanfront shack next to campus with seafood literally just off the boat. It was the best shellfish in China, better than in southern provinces because the seafood is meatier in cold waters.[8] I asked about the kosher students and what food they might enjoy. Not much of a practical problem, K. *shuji* said: We don't have any Jewish students. I asked about Muslim students on campus; our mouthwatering shrimp and crab might be considered *haram* by Muslims. K. *shuji* said not to worry, we will have a *halal* section in the cafeteria, like other major universities in China. I was hooked. What a beautiful opportunity to help promote Confucianism in China, all the while respecting other traditions! K. *shuji*, it should be said, never once mentioned anything about the need to promote communism or the CCP's agenda.[9] He was a builder and this campus was his baby. His main concern was to make the university into a world-class academic institution. First, we needed a beautiful campus that would attract scholars from around the world. That was done. Next, we needed talented academics to do original and cutting-edge research. He hoped that I could help with that. Flattered, I said yes.[10] Eventually, K. *shuji* became a close friend and confidant. I admire his serenity, kindness, and hard-work ethic, and I turn to him whenever I have problems.

At lower levels of the institutional hierarchy, the psychological care aspect of the *shuji*'s work is even more evident. Each faculty, including mine, has several *shuji* who deal with nonacademic matters, meaning, more often than not, acting like a psychological counselor who aims to secure "diversity in harmony" (和 *he*) in the university setting and helping students to find work after they graduate. Some *shuji* are given quotas specifying how many students are expected to find work and are rewarded or penalized depending on their success in meeting those quotas. I do not mean to deny that there is a political aspect to the *shuji*'s work. Academic meetings are often preceded by *shuji* reading out ideological directives sent from above, though many professors use this time to check their cell phones and few seem to listen too intently.[11] I have no doubt some of the *shuji*'s work undermines academic freedom. In my faculty, perhaps because I'm a foreigner and not a member of the CCP, I rarely have anything to do with political work. I know of some incidents of academic censorship in my faculty (including censorship of my own works)[12] and there are probably incidents I don't know about, but I'm not asked to enforce it. Except once. I run a lecture series, titled *Jixia Luntan* (稷下论坛), which seeks inspiration from debates at the Jixia Academy in ancient China. We invite two distinguished academics to debate an issue from different perspectives, a debate that we record and plan to distribute and publish in book form. Once, I invited two professors from a leading university in China to debate (in Chinese) the theme "What Is Good Government?" As usual, my assistant went through the bureaucratic procedures to get approval and I did not ask about the details. The day before the lecture, however, I was informed that I should delete the poster for the lecture from my WeChat account because we hadn't obtained formal approval for the lecture. Nor could students attend the lecture. The problem, I was told informally, was that we were too close to one of the politically sensitive anniversaries. But I was not told to cancel the lecture. So I went ahead with the event. We hosted a dinner for the two visiting professors along with several young members of our faculty. The seafood was excellent, and our dinner was enlivened with Tsingdao (aka Qingdao) beer that's much higher quality than the Tsingdao beer outside of Qingdao (because the local beer is made from the water of Lao mountain). Then we went to the lecture room with the professors. I announced, "This is not a lecture," and I made a reference to René Magritte's famous surrealist painting of a pipe with the written words "*Ceci n'est pas une pipe*" (This is not a pipe) underneath. People laughed, and then we proceeded with the lectures and discussion, all of which was recorded. I know about a professor who normally comes to lectures with visiting professors to make sure that the material is not politically sensitive (he never interferes and I've never been made aware of any complaints in that respect). But he didn't come to the lecture that day. I paid the honoraria for the talks from my dean's fund rather than the faculty fund for lecturers. To avoid conflict, all had to pretend that there had been no lecture. Harmony secured.

I recognize that I may be shut out from much of the dirty work. It's not something I'm proud of. But most of the *shuji's* day-to-day work is not dirty. Quite the opposite: It involves, as Mao famously said, "serving the people." When Covid hit China, our various *shuji* led the fight to protect students and faculty from the dreaded disease. They worked day and night to design and implement regulations that protected us without unnecessary inconvenience (our faculty had a four-week lockdown in early 2022 and all the university *shuji* lived full time on campus during this period, away from their families). In comparison, I felt quite selfish, with my abstract academic pursuits that have only a tenuous connection to the good of the world. Like other academics, I'm vain and hope to be recognized for what I do. But our *shuji* spend most of their time doing other-regarding work, without any clear personal benefit. For the first few months of Covid crisis, one faculty *shuji* was so tired from the hard work to secure the health of teachers and students that I feared for his own health.

When things go wrong with people's lives, it's the *shuji*'s task to try to make things right. The work requires remarkable people skills, or high emotional intelligence (EQ), a term that's widely used in everyday Chinese discourse (in contrast, academics can often thrive with high IQ and not-so-high EQ). We had a tragic accident when our campus had just opened and K. *shuji* had to spend difficult days comforting the student's family. Then he had to redesign the campus to help prevent such accidents in the future. It's one reason our campus is one of the few in China that bars cars from the center.

Here's another confession. I developed strong negative feelings against a junior teacher in our faculty. He frequently attacked my work, and my alleged moral failures, on the faculty WeChat account. It was embarrassing for me, but I did not respond publicly, aware of the power imbalance. To my great relief, the teacher was offered a job elsewhere and left our faculty. But he was still on our faculty WeChat account and continued to send mean-spirited comments about my work in public. Finally, I'd had enough and ordered the administrator in charge of the group WeChat to delete him from the account, since he was no longer a member of our faculty. It was perhaps the first time (in five years!) that I used my authority to issue a direct order that I expected to be obeyed, without going through our collective leadership system. To my surprise, however, my order was vetoed by the faculty *shuji*. Outraged, I went to his office (next to mine) to ask for an explanation. I asked, why keep this teacher on the faculty WeChat account since he has left our university? It makes no sense! Another issue was left unstated. This teacher was overtly anti-communist. He hated the political system and openly stated his contempt with sarcastic comments shared with other faculty members. Surely, I thought to myself, the *shuji*, supposedly in charge of enforcing loyalty to the CCP, would jump at the opportunity to get rid of this politically troublesome former teacher. (These were private thoughts. I would never use politics to judge a faculty member in public, whatever politically incorrect thoughts might go through my mind.) Our *shuji* must have been aware of the teacher's political orientation since his messages were so public. So I was shocked by G. *shuji*'s reticence to delete this (former) teacher from our faculty WeChat account. Here's what our *shuji* said. First, we have other former teachers who remain on the faculty WeChat account and it would seem odd if we deleted one but not the others. Second, it may be more of a public issue if the teacher is deleted since he may try to cause a stink. I replied that this former teacher's presence on the faculty WeChat inhibits what we say. In my own case, I dare not post things for fear of his retribution. I'm sure other faculty members feel the same way. Our *shuji* listened to those arguments, but he still wouldn't change his mind. He said, Let's wait a bit. If this former teacher continues to post poisonous messages with no academic substance, then we can remove him. And that's just what happened a few weeks later.

The high EQ of the *shuji*, not surprisingly, transfers to other domains that require similar talents. Li Zhang's *Anxious China: Inner Revolution and Politics of Psychotherapy* is a fascinating account of the rise of psychotherapy in contemporary China. Zhang argues that new psychotherapeutic technologies in China draw on older forms of "thought work" and extend beyond the clinical sphere of treating mental illness into other social domains: "It is against the backdrop of a particularly socialist legacy, known as 'political thought work' [政治思想工作 *zhengzhi sixiang gongzuo*], or governing through ideology based on persuasion, that a new form of therapeutic governing based on 'kindly care' [关爱 *guan ai*] becomes appealing to Chinese workers, students, soldiers, and others." Political thought work is not just a matter of espousing communist propaganda: "It is important to note that effective political 'thought work' tends to take place in a more personal setting and has an affective dimension involving feelings, attitudes, and gestures of care." Today, thought work is even more detached from its original political mission: "Nowadays, it is common for someone to ask a friend or relative to help with thought work on another person, which may involve purely personal matters." Not only that. Many therapists today who help patients with personal problems used to do political thought work: "Even though their focus in cognitive behavioral therapy work today is no longer on political ideology or political persuasion but rather on promoting personal growth and tackling emotional problems and familial troubles, the communication skills they learned from previous 'thought work' can be applied to talk therapy." Work as *shuji* and as therapist both require the same skills: "listening and building trust [is] far more important than persuasion and reasoning."[13]

In short, the *shuji* in university settings is not primarily a party secretary who blindly enforces party ideology against recalcitrant students and professors. Most of the work involves smoothing out social conflicts and promoting an atmosphere of "diversity in harmony" on campus. A better translation of university-level *shuji* would be "harmony secretary." I don't want to idealize the system. The university *shuji* system is deeply flawed. From an academic point of view, it's a bad idea to have one's work overseen by political commissars, even if little interference takes place in practice. I look forward to the day when academics in China are free to do their work without any political interference and judged solely by the meritocratic criteria of their academic peers.[14] At a minimum, this would mean getting rid of the system that invests *shuji* with substantial influence over academic hirings (and firings). But personal conflicts won't go away and we need some form of harmony secretaries in universities and other social institutions. We also need administrators who help to ensure that the university serves society, as opposed to "Western-style" university administrators whose main task is to serve professors who often do research that is completely detached from social needs. So here's my prediction: In China, the harmony secretary is here to stay, even if the whole political system collapses one day.

# 3

# On Collective Leadership

THE CULTURAL REVOLUTION, from 1966 to 1976, was a disastrous experience with radical populism and a crazed personality cult. To avoid a repeat experience of arbitrary one-man dictatorship at the top, Deng Xiaoping and other leaders established mechanisms meant to limit the possibility of a "bad emperor." Term limits for rulers were meant to help: As of 1982, the constitution stipulated that the president could not serve more than two consecutive terms. Deng Xiaoping continued to exercise substantial behind-the-scenes political power until his death in 1997, casting doubt on the practical implications of formal retirement. But Jiang Zemin and Hu Jintao retired after two five-year terms as president (and, more importantly, as party chief) and it did appear that term limits could effectively check the powers of the top political leader. That good news was short-lived: Chinese lawmakers abolished term limits for the president in 2018, effectively enabling President Xi to formally exercise political power for more than two five-year terms, reviving fears of an "emperor" gone rogue.[1] Fortunately, the other mechanism meant to limit arbitrary dictatorship at the top—collective leadership—continues to be in place. Collective leadership has changed over the years—one leader is now more equal than others—but the system still provides an important check on arbitrary decision-making by Numero Uno. If President Xi were to go senile, for example, we can expect that he'd be removed from the Standing Committee of the Politburo. What I say here is nothing new. What's less well-known is that political practices and mechanisms at the top filter down to lower levels of the Chinese bureaucracy, even without any formal orders to do so. When I assumed my deanship, it came as a surprise to learn that my own faculty at Shandong University is ruled by a collective leadership system. Let me discuss my experience with collective leadership in detail, and then I will draw implications for collective leadership at higher levels of government.

## A Powerful Dean?

My academic friends from the West seemed puzzled that I would want to take on an administrative job as dean of a large faculty in a fairly remote university. Productive academics in Western universities often dread the thought of administrative work because they prefer to have time to read and write. I recall a dinner at the house of a Stanford professor in Palo Alto. He received a call and jumped up in joy. He was elated because he had just been informed that he would *not* have to serve as head of his department. In China, it's a different story. Even leading academics compete for administrative jobs, the higher the better. Whatever the personal reasons, there are deeper roots that explain the difference. The Confucian ideal—the best life—is expressed by the saying "内圣外王" (*neisheng waiwang*), which means "sagely (inner) self-cultivation and humane (outer) kingship."[2] The second part of the ideal (outer kingship) was (imperfectly) instantiated by means of a complex bureaucratic system dating from China's first dynasty, with public officials competing for the right to serve the public *qua* bureaucrat. For more than two millennia, the highest honor was reserved for meritocratically selected and promoted public officials (with the notable exception of the Emperor himself). Of course, historical legacies cannot fully explain why academics compete to be university bureaucrats in China today; we also respond to incentives provided by contemporary institutions. But it's worth noting that salaries are typically much lower for high-ranking university bureaucrats (including university presidents and vice-presidents) than for leading academics in Chinese universities; I've often heard complaints of this nature from top university officials. Yet academics strive to be bureaucrats, an outlook that owes more to the Confucian heritage than the "communist" political system or the "capitalist" economic system.

Not surprisingly, such cultural legacies may be most evident in Shandong Province, the home of Confucian culture. My colleagues note with pride that many influential public officials in Chinese history came from Shandong, but we (Shangdongnese) never had an Emperor. The implication is that we are satisfied with being hard-working bureaucrats, but without engaging in the dirty politics that might be necessary to reach the very top. It's also noteworthy that the lucky number for license plates in Shandong is not "8," as in the rest of China (because "8" in Cantonese sounds like "wealth"), but "7" because of the expression "七上八下" (seven up, eight down), which refers to the promotion and demotion of public officials (on the assumption that if officials are not promoted by the age of 57, they are on the way to retirement at the age of 58).

As a card-carrying Confucian working and living in China, I was influenced by such concerns. Surely a full life involves serving the public in some capacity, and service as a university bureaucrat is the closest I'd come to this ideal. As a foreign-born and foreign-looking professor, I felt it to be a special privilege to be put in charge of a large, politically sensitive faculty of Shandong's top university. My Chinese friends were generally supportive. Some enthusiastically predicted that I'd eventually be promoted to vice-president, and maybe even president, of a university. I modestly waved aside such concerns, but deep in my heart I saw myself in a few years as the first foreign-born president of a major Chinese university, worthy of a write-up in the *Globe and Mail*, if not the *New York Times*.

I officially assumed my post as dean on January 1, 2017. The news was huge in China and I became known beyond academic circles. Even before I began my job, I was interviewed by several leading newspapers and TV shows to the point that strangers would recognize me on the streets of my village, Aoshanwei. It felt a bit odd becoming a minor star as a result of a new administrative position rather than the books I had authored (all of which had been translated into Chinese), but it helped my work to become better-known in China. I was repeatedly told by my Chinese friends that I needed a platform (平台) to communicate my views. It's not enough to be a professor at a famous university like Tsinghua. Nobody would listen unless I had some sort of administrative post that people know and respect. And the title dean (院长) is such a title: It sounds impressive in Chinese (when I'm introduced as dean, people's eyes light up, and I'm granted a new measure of respect).[3] Of course, I'd still like to think my main motivation was the as-yet-unfulfilled desire to serve others. I felt my life had been overly self-regarding so far, even within the family context, where I didn't do much work for loved ones. A fully actualized life involves use of the other-regarding reflex, and I was keen to put it to use.

When asked by media outlets why I wanted to serve as dean, my explanations were not so pompous sounding. I said that I could help the university with its mission to teach and promote Confucianism. It makes sense for the province's premier university to take pride in its Confucian heritage while being open to other influences and striving for diversity of perspectives. Also, I could help our faculty to internationalize by developing links with universities abroad, and our students and teachers could get more academic experience in other countries. I could draw on academic contacts abroad forged over the past three decades, encourage leading academics from around the world to give talks and participate in international conferences at Shandong University. I'd also try to attract global talent to teach in our faculty. My dual, seemingly contradictory (but sensible), mission would be to localize by promoting "our" Confucian culture and internationalize by means of more interaction with foreign faculty. And my position as dean could help to realize this double mission. My superiors told me that the dean has the power to shape the faculty in Chinese universities, unlike universities in the West, where the dean is often expected to serve as a kind of neutral, fair-minded umpire among (frequently warring) factions. In the Chinese system, I was told, the dean gets his way (院长说了算 *yuanzhang shuole suan*).

My mission to serve the people (unimpeded by the people) was soon served with a heavily polluted dose of reality. When I started work as dean, our faculty was in the process of moving from Jinan—the capital city of Shandong Province, deep in the interior—to Qingdao, the beautiful coastal city more than 350 kilometers away (more precisely, to tiny Aoshanwei, about one hour from Qingdao). In Jinan, the pollution was off the charts, with a PM 2.5 level of 650 (anything over 500 was once described as "crazy bad" by the U.S. embassy in Beijing). The air was literally unbreathable and left a metallic taste in my mouth for a week. Locals didn't seem to mind that much: They wore masks to ward off the pollution, but some tough-looking guys took them off to smoke cigarettes (I'm surprised no one came up with the idea of masks with holes for cigarette smoking). The mask wearing that proved to be necessary in the early days of the Covid scare did not come as a culture shock to the people of Jinan.

I started my job with a self-recruited assistant—formerly my undergraduate student at Tsinghua University—because my post did not include, surprisingly, an assistant (I was assigned a talented young teacher to help, but it seemed inappropriate to ask him to handle administrative matters). My assistant helped me to navigate the bureaucratic obstacles to normal life, such as opening a banking account with a form that had only two choices for foreigners: 美国人 (*meiguoren*, American) and 非美国人 (*fei meiguoren*, non-American).[4] My first request as dean was to put an air purifier in our hotel rooms. I was swiftly provided with a purifier, but my assistant did not get one. I once again asked the lead administrator in our faculty for help. She said, It's complicated owing to the tightening of regulations due to the anti-corruption campaign. I replied that it was a matter of survival; it had nothing to do corruption. She assured me that she would look into it further ("研究, 研究" *yanjiu yanjiu*). It took three days of repeated requests in the midst of life-threatening pollution for my assistant to get an air purifier for her hotel room. I learned the first lesson of a complex bureaucracy: The mother of all powers is the power to delay.

I was told in the first week that there were two important meetings: The faculty leaders' committee decides on major issues affecting the faculty and the academic committee decides on strictly academic matters such as whom to hire and promote (we had not yet developed a system to fire people, and five years on, we have yet to fire a single professor). The faculty leaders' committee consisted of four vice-deans (all male), three party secretaries, the lead administrator mentioned earlier, and myself. I was asked to sit in the middle, between the executive vice-dean and the faculty party secretary. I was told, half-jokingly, that it was a system of collective leadership. The meeting was scheduled at 8 a.m., ridiculously early from my perspective, as I had yet to break my graduate school habit of going to bed late and waking up late, with broken sleep in between. There was no written agenda and nothing was circulated beforehand.

I was asked to speak first. I said that I would listen to the others before venturing my own views. Each member of the faculty leaders' committee spoke for about fifteen minutes about their particular area of jurisdiction (one vice-dean was in charge of undergraduate education, another in charge of graduate education, another in charge of research, etc.), summarizing their work over the previous two weeks or so. Most of the discussion centered on the move: which tables and chairs to move to Qingdao, who should get which office in our new building, and how to accommodate the requests to limit office space as a result of the anti-corruption campaign. There were clear differences between leaders from Qingdao and Jinan. I thought that the decision to move from Jinan, with its hot and humid weather, heavy traffic, ugly architecture, and off-the-charts pollution to our new campus near Qingdao, with its clear air, beautiful beaches, and stunning Lao mountain in the background, should be, as the former CIA director George Tenet allegedly said about the existence of weapons of mass destruction in Saddam Hussein's Iraq, a "slam dunk." But professors with young children and elderly parents in Jinan were reluctant to move, and some couples might suffer from working in different cities: I was told that when China's "Oil University" (中国石油大学) split its campus into two cities, the divorce rate went up by 30 percent (I contributed to a similarly unhappy statistic at my university three years later).

Some of the differences seemed to date from the Warring States period, when Jinan was part of the Lu state (home of Confucianism) and Qingdao was a tiny fishing village in the state of Qi, more famous for its trading prowess. I was told (privately) that our faculty has more professors from the coastal cities of the former Qi state because there are more protein and calories in the fish they consumed, whereas the rest of the province was malnourished when the national university entrance examinations (*gaokao*) resumed in the late 1970s. More than 60 percent of the successful exam takers from Shandong for the first few years of the *gaokao* came from the coastal areas; hence, the Qi people were disproportionately put on the road to academia. But the Lu faction in our faculty seemed to think the move represented a decline in our "level of civilization."[5] There was no dispute about the move itself: It had been decided by the higher-ups. But we argued about timing, what to bring, and who should get what offices. At one point, the debate became so heated that one faculty leader stormed out of the meeting. Then I was asked to make decisions. I had nothing to say. For one thing, I was not used to the various Shandong accents, so I missed some crucial details. Second, I had no idea how to decide between conflicting viewpoints because I did not know the people involved (we have about eighty professors in our faculty) or the regulations governing matters of controversy. Finally, our strikingly handsome executive vice-dean C. spoke. What authority! He mastered all the details, did his best to include the suggestions of other leaders, and came up with ideas that none had mentioned before. When he spoke, all fell silent and agreed to his suggestions. Not only did they seem fair and well-thought-out but also he spoke with humility and humor. I had my first inkling about who was the real leader of our faculty.

After four hours, the meeting came to an end. I was shell-shocked, and so was my assistant, who felt completely *dépaysé* coming from Beijing.[6] She knew about the bureaucratic culture of Shandong but had not anticipated the seemingly endless discussions and invocation of baffling regulations. I had been to a few faculty meetings at Tsinghua University, but none lasted more than an hour or so. In Hong Kong, the meetings were even more efficient, with detailed notes distributed in advance that could be studied before the meeting. I was determined to streamline our meetings and to promote more efficiency in our faculty. My first request was to reschedule the next meeting for the afternoon. I was informed that this was impossible because other leaders had teaching obligations and university-level meetings in the afternoon, but we could move the start time to 8:30 a.m. I jokingly told my assistant that it was my first victory. She replied that it might be my only victory. Little did I know it wasn't such a joke.

The next day, we had a meeting of the academic committee. It consisted of fourteen members who had equal voting rights regarding hiring and promotion decisions, though the faculty decisions also needed to be approved by higher-level university authorities. I realized that this was an all-important committee, though I also realized that I wouldn't have much influence. Worse, I was told that I could not formally join the committee because the regulations were somewhat complicated for new faculty members. But I could participate as a non-voting member and I'd soon be allowed to join. It took two and a half years for me to be formally appointed to the academic committee.

A few months into the job, I realized that I was out of my depth. I was not appointed to any university-level committee (unlike other deans) and had yet to meet our university president one-on-one (I had asked for a meeting but it never materialized). Far from harboring hopes of promotion, I feared that I might not be able to fulfill my task as dean. In the first few months, I said I'd meet with all the teachers in our faculty for one-on-one discussion about what works and what doesn't and to ask for suggestions about how to move forward.[7] But it was hard to get appointments because several faculty members were living in Jinan when I was in Qingdao and vice versa. I did meet with some professors. To my pleasant surprise, there was support for reinstating a compulsory first-year course in political theory, with more content from the Confucian tradition. When I raised this suggestion to faculty leaders, however, it was the first time I saw faces change to less-than-friendly expressions. I was told that it's very difficult to change the course curriculum, and numerous bureaucratic obstacles were raised. I got the message and realized that I'd make no progress pushing for changes to our curriculum. Another time, I tried to organize another international conference on Confucian political theory, but the conference was vetoed at the last minute by the Ministry of Education for political reasons and, to my great embarrassment, I had to ask international participants to cancel. I realized that it would be very difficult to attract international faculty who didn't speak Chinese because of our remote location and lack of English-language facilities on campus. My mission to Confucianize and internationalize had to take a back seat to more seemingly mundane concerns such as providing professors with more office space, time for research, and higher salaries.

Such concerns were discussed during our faculty meetings, but I continued to lack sufficient local knowledge to put forward informed suggestions. The faculty meetings continued to drag on for four hours, with seemingly endless talk and our executive vice-dean as the unofficial decider-in-chief. I did put forward suggestions for streamlining the meetings. I requested that our talk be limited to discussing problems that needed to be solved rather than reporting on work done. I asked faculty leaders to submit written reports beforehand so we needn't spend so much time reviewing them at the meetings. My suggestions had limited effect. A few leaders submitted reports, but I was told unofficially that it was too time-consuming to prepare written material. Plus, many issues came up at the last minute. And it was not always easy to identify what counts as a problem that needed to be solved versus work done: The whole point of going over work done is to let others identify potential problems. Eventually, things returned to the *status quo ante*. I realized that most faculty leaders enjoyed such lengthy meetings. I also realized that I was not cut out to be a minor bureaucrat in Shandong Province.

About one year later, I was told that our super-talented executive vice-dean had been promoted to vice-president of Shandong University's Qingdao campus. To my embarrassment, I reacted by expressing alarm to our party secretary (I had no time to digest the information: I was told the news just before being asked to meet with members of our university's Organization Department to discuss the promotion). It's not because I was jealous (I had long ago given up aspirations to being promoted within the university hierarchy). I worried that our faculty might collapse without our executive vice-dean. I certainly didn't feel I could take over the job of de facto decider-in-chief and I had no idea who might do so. Luckily, I recovered my wits in time for the meeting with the Organization Department. I expressed my admiration for our executive vice-dean and said—with all sincerity—that he was brilliant at managing people as well as dealing with academic controversies in a fair way, and I could not think of a better person to serve as a high-level university leader.[8]

At the next faculty leaders' meeting, I fought hard to give up the central seat to our soon-to-be vice-president. But he insisted on letting me occupy the central seat. We'd have many such mock fights about who should occupy the key position at faculty meetings, and he usually "won" by guiding me to the central seat. I did learn to fight harder and I occasionally "won" by arriving early, occupying the less prestigious seat, and forcing him to occupy the central seat. To my surprise (and relief), our executive vice-dean kept his old position and continued to serve on the faculty leaders' committee even while serving as vice-president of our campus. I did worry about his health—the double job seemed to be so exhausting—and felt guilty that I could not (or would not) do more.

To be fair (to myself), I did eventually learn some tricks of the trade. If I had ideas for how to improve our faculty, it was best to build on existing structures rather than try to change them. I learned that we cannot promote Confucianism without trained teachers. I'd never get anywhere by asking, much less forcing, our faculty to teach more Confucianism if they have no interest or expertise in the topic. But I could hire new teachers with the relevant background. Here I had some success.[9] In my first year, I helped to hire a brilliant professor I had known since his undergraduate days at Peking University in the mid-1990s, when he had presented me with a tiny pocket-sized copy of the *Analects of Confucius* and told me that he was a seventy-sixth-generation descendant of Confucius; it was the first time I learned of the distinguished Kong family tree.[10] Professor K., born and bred in Qufu, was trained in both Western intellectual history and Confucian ethics and could draw insightful comparisons that engaged both foreign and Chinese students. He is a charismatic teacher and students love him. Professor K. quickly ascended in the administrative hierarchy and was made vice-dean and became a key member of our collective leadership. He helped to hire more teachers who could teach the history and philosophy of Confucianism, and I came to realize that we'd slowly make more headway "Confucianizing" our faculty largely through his efforts.[11] On a personal level, he is my drinking partner and, like other Shandong "哥们" (brothers), we hold hands and share intimacies that we often forget the next morning due to excessive imbibition.[12]

As far as internationalization, I eventually found my niche, with the support of other leaders. I co-organized a summer school for our students in Norway comparing East Asian and Nordic cultures. I helped some of our teachers to go abroad on sabbatical. I organized an international conference comparing ancient Indian and ancient Chinese international political thought. I signed several memoranda for cooperation with foreign universities. And I sponsored several lecturers from China and abroad, with huge crowds of students hungry for knowledge. But internationalization came to a crashing halt with Covid, and the best I could do since early 2020 was to hold on to what we had, such as fighting hard for our university to grant travel authorization for our foreign faculty stuck abroad (they were eventually granted permission for reentry after two years of trying).

I also learned to navigate, to a certain extent, the system of collective leadership, especially when we dealt with international issues because it was assumed (often wrongly) that my background provided special expertise. In one case, two of our foreign students were caught smoking drugs. I asked about the drug and was told it was marijuana. My colleagues could tell from my facial expression that I didn't think it was a big deal. Someone said that it's common in foreign universities and I agreed, without mentioning my own rich experience as an undergraduate with what we used to call extracurricular activities. I argued for the lightest possible punishment: a fine of 500 rmb (U.S.$78) and a warning. My colleagues ultimately agreed, if only because a big public stink would look bad for our faculty and affect our ability to recruit students from abroad. Another time, one of our foreign faculty got into trouble with students during an online course. He was abroad due to Covid and it was his first online course. The teacher was upset that some students sent WeChat messages to friends during his talk (he could tell from their videos) and that somebody was recording his talk without his permission. He lost his cool, swore on air, and made the students feel terrible. Shandong University students typically have great respect for teachers, but two-thirds of the students signed a petition asking for dismissal of the offending teacher (a minority of the students supported the teacher, who was famous for being strict but devoted to students, perhaps more so than any other teacher in our faculty). It was a big crisis and I was called in for discussion by our party secretary. I have great respect for Shandong University students but I thought they went too far (disclosure: the teacher is a dear friend). So a few leaders informally came up with what I thought was a good compromise: We'd appoint another teacher for the two-thirds of the students who signed the petition so that they could take the same class with another teacher, and the rest could continue with the original teacher. The offending teacher realized that he had gone too far and he wrote a sincere apology to the students.

But the students rejected the compromise: Those who left the class feared retaliation in future classes (even though we didn't tell the offending teacher which students had signed the petition), and they said the class shouldn't be split up because peer assessment, based on experience and friendships, was an important standard for student leaders who wanted to join the CCP. So we had to call a formal meeting with leaders to collectively deliberate about the possibility of an outcome that would be fair and acceptable to all sides. Nobody argued for sacking the offending teacher. But some argued for depriving him of teaching that semester along with a formal admonition and a salary cut. I argued for a "light" punishment in the form of depriving him of the right to teach that course but he could continue to teach his other courses. We went through several rounds of arguments and eventually my suggestion won out.

Beyond that, however, I cannot claim much success. In my own mind, I'd failed to live up to my initial expectations. Our university would not become known as a model Confucian university in the foreseeable future and internationalization would need to take a back seat to other concerns. The deepest problem was not linguistic or cultural or political. We are supposed to be always on call and be ready for four-hour meetings with other leaders on short notice. I just didn't have the energy for the job.[13]

## An Ideal Form of Collective Leadership?

Whatever my personal failures, I do see the merits of collective leadership as an institution. I do not mean to imply that collective leadership in my faculty is ideal. Nor do I mean to imply that what we do is similar to the workings of collective leadership in the Standing Committee of the Politburo (I have no way of knowing how things work at the highest levels of government because there is no transparency). But perhaps I can draw some implications from my own experience with a kind of collective leadership about what works and what doesn't that may also be relevant for evaluating its workings at higher levels of government. Here goes.

(1) *Hard work.* In my earlier book *The China Model*—published before I became dean—I drew on academic studies to put forward suggestions about which qualities matter for public officials in the context of large, peaceful, and modernizing political meritocracies. I concluded that IQ, EQ, and virtue (in the sense of a willingness to serve the public and not misuse public funds for one's personal benefit) are important qualities.[14] Now I can see what was missing from my list: the capacity for hard work.[15] I have deep admiration for fellow leaders in my faculty not just because I think they have above-average IQ, EQ, and virtue, but also because they work so hard and tirelessly for the good of the faculty. My biggest failure as dean is that I lack this capacity for hard work serving other people. So, what are the implications for collective leadership at higher levels of government? If all the leaders work hard for the good of the political community, we can expect that the system is more likely to work well. Conversely, if some leaders are lazy, or just going through the motions, as seems to have been the case in the latter stages of the Soviet Union, we can expect that the political system is in trouble. In a famous comment published in the *Wall Street Journal* in 2015, the China watcher David Shambaugh predicted "The Coming Chinese Crack-Up" partly because political authority had become "ossified" and "even many regime loyalists are just going through the motions."[16] My experience with collective leadership at Shandong University suggests otherwise, and the few public

officials I do know at higher levels of government work tirelessly trying to solve problems. I was the glaring exception. That's an important reason to be optimistic about the future of China's political system.

(2) *Concern with efficiency.* Our main problem is that meetings dragged on way too long. But it's both possible and desirable to strive for more efficiency. Discussion in collective leadership should be focused on problems rather than reports of work already accomplished. Small talk should be minimized. The number of leaders should be capped: In my experience, if each person talks for about fifteen minutes, then with further deliberations, it makes for extremely long meetings. So about seven or eight collective leaders should be the maximum, with each leader having a chance to talk from his or her perspective about problems that need to be solved. I do not know how things work at the highest levels of government, but with seven to nine leaders in the Standing Committee of the Politburo, the numbers seem about right from an efficiency standpoint.

(3) *Inequality is good.* If all the leaders are equals, it will be difficult to get things done. Discussion will be prolonged and conflicting points of view will be hard to resolve, and if they are resolved by majority vote rather than informal consensus, voting factions may emerge and some leaders are likely to be profoundly dissatisfied. A division of labor is necessary for purposes of efficiency, but if the division of labor is rigidly equal, with each leader in charge of an area and possessing de facto veto power over decisions affecting that area, it will be difficult to make hard decisions for the overall good. There is a need for a "first among equals" leader who has the ability to consider different perspectives and who has the moral if not formal authority to be decider-in-chief. I regret to report that I was not such a leader. Fortunately, our executive vice-dean instantiated that role.

He was a good listener who could gently persuade other leaders to come around to his middle ground. Moreover, he had extensive experience with a large network of friends in the university who trusted him and respected his judgment. In a widely cited article titled "Getting Ahead in the Communist Party," Victor Shih and his collaborators argued that the Chinese political system is not meritocratic at higher levels of government because Central Committee members were promoted on the basis of subjective factors such as "factional ties" rather than the ability to deliver economic growth.[17] But the standard for political meritocracy may legitimately differ at higher levels of government. At lower levels of government, it may be important to promote officials according to more objective criteria such as the ability to promote economic growth. At higher levels, however, it's a different story. If a leader has accumulated a large number of trusted friends over the course of a decades-long ascent to power, those friends are likely to help implement his or her decisions. At the very top, it means that he or she is more likely to be "first among equals" in the collective leadership system and it will be easier to get things done for the good of the community. When I give talks on Chinese-style political meritocracy and I'm asked why President Xi was selected as Numero Uno instead of other highly competent and hard-working leaders, I say, only half-jokingly, "朋友多" (he has lots of friends).[18]

(4) *Need for free expression and critical viewpoints.* A clear benefit of collective leadership is that diverse perspectives can inform the policy-making process. But it won't work well if the top leader doesn't take into account other perspectives. For collective leadership to work well, all leaders should feel free to express dissent. No human leader, no matter how great, can have a good grasp of all matters of government in a modern,

complex society such as China, and he or she is likely to have some mistaken views that need to be corrected. So other leaders in the collective leadership have an obligation to criticize mistaken views, even (especially) if they come from the "first among equals." Confucius himself was asked for one saying that would destroy the state, and he responded "if a ruler is deficient and no one contradicted him."[19] In my faculty, I'm pleased to report that our decider-in-chief is indeed a good listener who is willing to change his views in response to the criticisms of others. That's why I'm confident about the future of our faculty. At higher levels of government, however, I'm not so confident. Do the other six members of the Standing Committee present alternative possibilities and criticize the views of President Xi when they deliberate about policy proposals? I hope so, but it's blind hope. Given that President Xi is portrayed in the official media as an all-knowing ruler who has made great intellectual contributions to political theory and economic thinking, it does make one wonder. In response to recent foreign policy blunders, a leading China analyst concludes, "What [Xi] has now and will likely have in the future is a group of yes men."[20] It's also worrisome that President Xi has sought to impose a conception of the good life that may be appropriate for patriotic public officials—we are supposed to work hard and struggle for the common good—on artists and others who may be legitimately motivated by different conceptions of the good, such as the desire to create works of beauty.[21] Imperial China did not have a system of collective leadership, but two court historians (史官)—one of whom was in charge of monitoring the Emperor's actions, the other the Emperor's words—served as informal checks on the Emperor's power to make crazy decisions because the Emperor knew that his words and actions would be recorded for posterity.[22] It's not hard to think of contemporary equivalents—say, the deliberations of the Standing Committee could be filmed and publicly released in fifty years. Such mechanisms could serve as encouragement for the supreme leader to show that he recognizes his limitations and takes seriously alternative perspectives and for his colleagues to prove that they stand up to mistaken views and proposals. But it's more blind hope . . .

# 4

# What's Wrong with Corruption?

IN CHINA, corruption is the mother of all political evils. From a Confucian perspective, the best life involves serving the community *qua* public official and, conversely, the worst life involves misuse of public funds for private or family purposes. Such ideas influence history. Why did the Ming Dynasty collapse? Why did the Qing Dynasty collapse? There are many reasons, but the explosive growth of corruption had an important role to play in undermining the legitimacy of these long-lasting dynasties. And why did the CCP defeat the KMT in China's civil war? It wasn't due to superior weaponry. An important reason is that the CCP succeeded in winning the people's support, mainly because it was viewed as less corrupt and more willing to serve the people. Of course, these sweeping claims about Chinese history need to be qualified. Historians can debate complexities. For CCP leaders, however, such facts, or interpretations of facts, influence what they say and do.

In the first three decades of CCP rule, corruption was not the main problem. Millions of people perished in manmade famines and cruel persecution of perceived class enemies, but political leaders, including Chairman Mao himself, seemed drunk on power rather than hungry for money. Starting in the late

1970s, however, market-based economic reforms enriched the country, and public officials eagerly sought a cut. Still, the country moved forward and hundreds of millions were lifted out of poverty. By the turn of the millennium, however, corruption began to get out of hand. Poll after poll showed that corruption was viewed as an important problem by the Chinese public. It was often necessary to pay bribes to get into good schools or access decent health care. The system was viewed as particularly unfair by those (i.e., the majority) without wealth or political connections. That's not to say the whole system was viewed as irredeemably corrupt. There were "islands of probity" that could be used as the basis for improvement of the rest of the system.[1] Most notably, the national examination system (高考 gaokao), whatever its flaws, was viewed as a relatively fair and corruption-free way of deciding who gets into which university. And mid- to high-level public officials were viewed as more capable and less corrupt than lower-level public officials. Whatever the reality, lower-level corruption was more "in your face" and thus the direct target of the people's ire.

China's leaders openly recognized that corruption was inflaming public attitudes to the point of endangering the legitimacy of the political system. Former president Hu Jintao warned that corruption "could prove fatal to the party, and even cause the collapse of the party and the fall of the state," and his predecessor Jiang Zemin said that "corruption is the cancer in the body of the party and the state. If we let it be, our party, our political power and our socialist modernization cause will be doomed."[2] In response, they launched half-hearted anti-corruption campaigns, but things seemed only to get worse.

When Xi Jinping assumed the presidency in 2012, corruption had reached a tipping point and Xi made combating corruption the government's top priority.[3] The government launched what has turned out to be the longest and most systematic anti-corruption campaign in Communist Party history. As of 2018, more than one million officials had been punished for corruption, including a dozen high-ranking military officers, several senior executives of state-owned companies, and five national leaders. Cynical observers claim that the whole thing is a means of going after political enemies, but what distinguishes this anti-corruption drive from previous ones is that it also creates many political enemies, which seems irrational from the point of view of political self-preservation.

Whatever the motivation, the effect is clear: The anti-corruption drive has worked.[4] Anybody who has dealt with public officials has noticed the changes. Corrupt practices are now almost universally frowned on. The profits of companies are up because there's no longer a need to pay extras to public officials. Ordinary citizens perceive the system as less unfair because it's now possible to access public services without paying bribes and gifts to bureaucrats. Most surprising, the anti-corruption drive has been successful without the mechanisms designed to limit abuses of power in liberal democracies: competitive elections, a free press, and independent anti-corruption agencies. China's Leninist-inspired political system rules out such mechanisms and allows for abuses such as indefinite detention without trial.

But Leninism isn't the whole story. The means employed owe much to China's own Legalist tradition (法家 *fajia*). In conversation with public officials, including high-ranking leaders, the language of Legalism is frequently invoked to justify the anti-corruption drive. Legalism—meaning rule *by* law rather than rule *of* law—is China's alternative to "Confucian compassion": When faced with serious threats to their power or China's social order, rulers in Beijing have often relied on Legalist methods that justify heavy-handed state power and harsh punishments to secure social order.

It has worked, at least in the short term. Inspired by Legalism, the self-proclaimed First Emperor of Qin united China in the late third century BCE. But the Qin empire lasted for only fifteen years—the shortest-lived major dynasty in Chinese history—and Emperor Qin went down in history as a cruel dictator. The downsides of what we might term "Leninist legalism" are equally evident in today's anti-corruption drive. It's not just that public officials think twice before engaging in corrupt practices. They think almost all the time about what can go wrong, to the point that decision-making has become virtually paralyzed. The procedures for using public funds have become bafflingly complex and punitive, and it's safer not to spend money. The costs are huge, and growing. China's success over the past four decades is partly explained by the fact that government officials were encouraged to experiment and innovate, thus helping to propel China's reforms. But ultra-cautious behavior from the government means that innovative officials won't get promoted and problems won't get fixed.[5]

The coronavirus crisis shows that paralyzing public officials can be literally deadly. Hundreds of lives were lost because public officials failed to react swiftly to the crisis. Instead, local officials muzzled "whistleblowers" who warned about a mysterious SARS-like virus in late December 2019, most famously Dr. Li Wenliang, who succumbed to the deadly virus two months later at the age of thirty-four. Dr. Li's death led to an outpouring of anger on social media. If the corrupt official was the bane of the Chinese public before the anti-corruption campaign, today it's the do-nothing official who blindly sticks to the rules and cares for nothing other than pleasing higher-ups.

Equally serious, the anti-corruption drive has created huge numbers of political enemies who may be rooting for the downfall of the leaders, if not the whole political system. For every high-level public official brought down by the anti-corruption drive, there may be dozens of allies and subordinates who lose their prospects of mobility in an ultra-competitive, decades-long race to the apex of political power. The "losers" in the anti-corruption drive blame China's rulers for their predicament. These real enemies make the leaders even more paranoid than usual and lead the government to ramp up censorship and further curb civil and political rights. So, it isn't just the political outcasts who feel estranged from the system but also intellectuals and artists, who object to curbs on what they do, as well as business people who worry about political stability and flee abroad with their assets.

With yet more social dissatisfaction among elites, leaders further clamp down on real and potential dissent. Knowing that their enemies are waiting to pounce, the current leaders are even less likely to give up power (elderly leaders may not worry so much about their own fate because they will soon "visit Karl Marx," but they worry about their children and family members). So, it's a vicious circle of Legalist means and political repression. Ironically, the most efficient and effective drive to limit abuses of power in recent Chinese history (in the form of the anti-corruption campaign) may also have led the leaders of the campaign to remove the most important constraints on their own power (in the form of term and age limits).

When I assumed "power" as a minor bureaucrat in January 2017, it was at the height of the anti-corruption drive. At the time, I was completely supportive of the effort to wipe out corruption. A friend joked that I missed out on the "good old corrupt days." In the past, I could have invited guests to lavish meals, including exclusive "white liquor" (白酒 *bai jiu*), all at public expense, and then treated my guests to karaoke with beautiful hostesses. I'd have my own chauffeur. In reality, however, it's unlikely that a foreign citizen would have been offered my job with access to the seemingly corrupt side benefits. From a public point of view, I recognized the necessity of the anti-corruption drive. Plus, I couldn't complain. I was offered a good salary by Chinese standards, along with subsidized accommodation with a view of the sea right next to our beautiful new campus. And my colleagues were kind and supportive.

Still, I soon experienced the downside of the anti-corruption drive. Notwithstanding official rhetoric about the need for less "bureaucratic formalism," the rules governing everyday life became more rigid. Before I took the job, I had been promised a large office. But now, the offices of university deans were strictly limited by regulations issued from the central government: For some bureaucratic reason, they were even smaller than the offices of some ordinary professors. I didn't mind too much because most of my books that really take up space were at home. But it was a bit embarrassing when I had to greet visitors to my faculty who expected something grander. Sometimes I'd greet visitors in a larger public office on my floor. Or else we'd just meet in our university library. It's a stunning twelve-story building—the largest library in Asia (in terms of floor space, not number of books)—and I'd take them to the top floor to get a view of the sea, the mountains, and our university buildings. To foreign guests, I'd have to explain the whole context of the anti-corruption campaign, pointing out that our party secretary's office was no larger than mine.

The excessive Legalism really got on my nerves when I hosted meals. We could not order meals that cost more than 98 rmb per person (about U.S.$15). We had to write down the name of every dish we ordered and we had to pay for our own liquor. I didn't have my own credit card or university account for inviting guests, and it was always confusing whether I had the authority to sign for the bill. Mealtime became a boring bureaucratic chore, almost the opposite of what it had been in the fun-filled corrupt days. It became a bit tiring, and after a while I began to host fewer meals, acting like those other bureaucrats who keep their heads down for fear of getting them chopped off.

Worse, the politically paranoid atmosphere affected our academic work. It's not just that bureaucrats became more conservative and risk averse. More and more subjects in political science were treated as politically sensitive, and the space for pure academic research narrowed. Liberal-minded colleagues who used to research topics such as public contestation and village elections needed to find new topics. Even seemingly innocuous "pro-Chinese" subjects were off limits. I tried to organize an international conference on the theme of "*tianxia*"—an ideal of global governance rooted in Chinese tradition—that was vetoed at the last minute by the Ministry of Education. I had to send embarrassed apologies to our invited guests from abroad, only vaguely alluding to the reason for the cancellation. Although I was supposed to help internationalize our faculty, I had hit a wall created by the paranoid political system.

In retrospect, it may have been a mistake to rely almost exclusively on Legalist means to combat corruption. Legalism can bring short-term political success, but it can also lead to long-term doom, similar to the fate of the Qin Dynasty. Chinese history does point to other possibilities, including amnesties for corrupt officials. As the current anti-corruption drive was getting under way, reformers argued that a general amnesty be granted to all corrupt officials, with serious policing of the boundaries between private and public, and resources provided to allow them to start afresh. To deal with the买官 *mai guan* (buying of government posts) problem, public posts could have been distributed by lottery once officials pass a certain level of qualification, as was done under Emperor Wanli. But it's too late to start over.

What can be done is to wind down the anti-corruption drive. Vice-President Wang Qishan—who led the anti-corruption drive—said that the drive will need to move from an initial deterrent stage to a point where the idea of acting corruptly would not even occur to officials as they went about their business. The next stage can't rely primarily on fear of punishment. It must rely on measures that reduce the incentives for corruption, including a clearer separation of economic and political power and higher salaries for public officials.[6] It also matters what officials do when nobody is looking: Moral education in the Confucian classics can help to change mind-sets in the long term. The central authorities should put more trust in talented public officials with good track records of serving the public. Any political system must balance constraining government officials from doing bad and empowering them to do good, and the balance in China needs to swing back to the latter. There may be too few constraints on the power of top leaders, but there are too many constraints on the others.

Luckily, the anti-corruption drive began to wind down a couple of years later. Notwithstanding the Wuhan debacle, there are glimmers of hope. At my university, we began to feel a somewhat more relaxed atmosphere. It was no longer necessary to write down the name of every dish I ordered to claim reimbursement for faculty meals. To the great relief of public officials from Shandong Province, the constraints on drinking alcohol at mealtime have been relaxed. I could order cheap beer at public expense (I never found out if there was an official change of policy, nor did I ask). Banquets became fun once again. Salaries for teachers increased. We felt more trust and less fear.

In the country as a whole, fewer officials have been punished for corruption and there is increased emphasis on moral education for public officials, including more teaching of Confucian-style values at Communist schools for cadres. With more reliance on Confucian self-regulation to curb corruption, China's leaders will have fewer political enemies, and they can relax a bit and do what they are supposed to do—namely, to serve the people. Whether it's too late to save the political system remains to be seen.[7]

# 5

# Drinking without Limits

CONFUCIUS, LIKE ARISTOTLE, favored a moderate approach to life: "The Middle Way is the highest level of virtue" (*Analects* 6.29). With one notable exception: "only with regard to alcohol did [Confucius] set no limits" (*Analects* 10.8). According to Edward Slingerland, "the fact that Confucius could drink to his heart's content but never became unruly is a sign of his sagehood."[1] Confucius himself was more modest in his self-assessment. He could "follow what [his] heart desired, without transgressing what was right" only at the age of seventy (*Analects* 2.4), with the implication that he transgressed what was right before then, perhaps after a few too many drinks. In any case, Confucius set the model for the Confucianized people of Shandong Province. Formal banquets are accompanied with endless toasts, and there is strong social pressure to demonstrate one's "drinking ability" (酒量). Not surprisingly, Shandong has the highest per capita alcohol consumption in China.[2]

As dean, I'm expected to host dinners for guests as well as for teachers, students, and visitors. Some dinners are more formal than others, but they all take the same form: As lead host, I sit at the "top" of a round table with a view of the door, and the others are seated around the table according to their level in the social hierarchy.[3] The meal is accompanied by frequent ritual-ized toasts and humorous speeches. After a few communal toasts, the local hosts (including myself) usually go around the table and do individual toasts with each guest. The effect is to produce a sense of bonding and the social hierarchies break down toward the end of the evening. I confess that it's my fa-vorite part of my "work" as dean.

Of course, heavy drinking has a downside. In less "civilized" parts of Shandong, women are often mistreated during the drinking process: In a widely publicized case in Jinan, a manager at Alibaba was accused of sexually assaulting an inebriated employee.[4] Subordinates feel pressure to drink to the point of oblivion: When the "boss" toasts an employee, it can be hard to refuse. In my case, I do not put pressure on reluctant partici-pants. Some people are allergic to alcohol and others don't enjoy drinking. Fine with me. But the social pressure can be self-induced. I invite my graduate students for celebratory meals on special occasions. One of my students, however, cannot hold his liquor very well and he feels bad about it. I tell him that it doesn't matter and he shouldn't try to keep up with the rest of us, but he tries to join the festivities nonetheless, with predictably unhappy results. He does seem to be making some "progress," in the sense that he can drink a few shots without passing out, though I'm not sure it's something to be proud of.

Overall, I'm pleased to report that things have changed for the better. Shandong is still the most patriarchal part of China, but there is more respect for women in university settings. No-body is forced to drink. At formal banquets, it is acceptable to replace fiery "white liquor" (白酒) with water and join the toasts with the "real" drinkers. Banquets end without incident, which wasn't true in the past. When I first visited Shandong Prov-ince about two decades ago, I participated in some banquets as a guest. To my shock, I'd be driven back to my hotel by heavily inebriated hosts. I feel lucky to be alive today. But many victims of drunk driving were not so lucky. People routinely ignored the norm against drunk driving, even though they knew deep down that it was the wrong thing to do. Today, it's a different story. There is a powerful prohibition against drunk driving, even without much of a police presence. We don't need to be reminded that it's the wrong thing to do. What happened? To understand more, let's go back in time.

## Drunk Driving in Beijing

One of China's lesser-known miracles is that driving habits have gone from terrible to decent, if not civil, in the span of a few decades. In the 1990s, it was still common to see cars plowing through red lights in the country's capital, necessitating the presence of human authority figures (police officers) who could control traffic flow, rendering the traffic signals all but useless. The traditional habit of trusting people but not technology in a quickly modernizing society had yet to be shed. Cars would switch lanes almost at random, putting bicyclists and pedestrians at risk of death every time they stepped out. The worst offenders were fancy cars with government license plates, who flouted the law with impunity, enraging local residents. The cars of the police who were supposed to enforce the law set the model for how to break it.

Things improved by the time I moved to Beijing in 2004. Drivers had more experience, and they obeyed traffic lights. Traffic was horrible and the skies were foggy with pollution, so it was impossible to drive fast (I confess that I didn't feel sorry for the Ferraris stuck in traffic jams). A few years later, in response to President Xi's anti-corruption drive, public officials were forced to ride in more modest cars and obey traffic rules. Policemen (I've yet to see a policewoman) did what they were supposed to do. Cameras installed at major intersections took photos of the license plates of cars that broke the rules, which made drivers much more cautious. What didn't change, however, was the habit of driving after drinking alcohol. It was still common practice and there was hardly any attempt to hide it, even though people knew it wasn't kosher. But the problem of drunk driving has also been brought under control over the past few years. How did they do it? The socialist tradition and Leninist politics don't offer much help. We need to go back to China's greatest political theorist—Xunzi (third century BCE)—for some insights.

Xunzi is widely regarded as one of the three founding fathers of Confucianism (along with Confucius and Mencius). He has been tainted because of his supposed influence on the Legalists, but his ideas had great influence on the actual politics of East Asian societies. His writings are clear and systematic, and he deliberately avoids utopian assumptions about human nature and society. In fact, he begins with the assumption that "human nature tends toward badness" (ch. 23).[5] If people follow their bodily natures and indulge their natural inclinations, aggressiveness and exploitation are sure to develop, resulting in cruel tyranny and poverty (ch. 19). Fortunately, that's not the end of the story. People can "become good by conscious exertion" (ch. 23). They can learn to contain their natural desires and enjoy the benefits of peaceful and cooperative social existence.

The key to transformation is ritual (ch. 23).[6] By learning and participating in rituals, people can learn to contain their desires, there will be a fit between people's actual desires and the goods available in society, and social peace and material well-being will result (ch. 19). Rituals provide bonds not based solely on kinship that allow people to partake of the benefits of social existence. But what exactly is ritual? Xunzi's account of ritual has seven features: (1) It is a social practice (as opposed to behavior involving only one person); (2) it is grounded in tradition (as opposed to newly invented social practices); (3) it involves both emotion and behavior (as opposed to paying behavioral lip service to social norms; an "empty ritual" is not a ritual in Xunzi's sense); (4) it involves different social groups and generates a sense of community among people with different power and status, hence benefiting both the powerful and the weak (as opposed to social practices that involve and benefit only one class of society); (5) it can be changed according to social context (as opposed to sticking rigidly to details that no longer mean anything to people); (6) it is socially legitimate (as opposed to practices that are not endorsed by society at large, such as blood oaths between criminal gangs); and (7) it is noncoercive (in contrast to legal punishments).[7]

The best kind of society, according to Xunzi, is regulated first and foremost by ritual. It is led by a "humane king" (王 *wang*), meaning a ruler who wins the hearts of the people and selects bureaucratic personnel based on ability and virtue. At home, the proper use of rituals, combined with effective policies that secure peace and prosperity, is key to leadership success: "One who cultivates ritual becomes a humane king; one who effectively exercises government becomes strong" (ch. 9). Setting a good model at home is necessary but not sufficient. The humane king can gain the hearts of those abroad by institutionalizing interstate rituals: "If you want to deal with the norms between small and large, strong and weak states to uphold them prudently, then rituals and customs must be especially diplomatic, the jade disks should be especially bright, and the diplomatic gifts particularly rich, the spokespersons should be gentlemen who write elegantly and speak wisely. If they keep people's interests at heart, who will be angry with them?" (ch. 10). Xunzi the political realist, however, recognizes that such humane rulers are few and far between.

The second-best kind of state is led by a "hegemon" (霸 ba) who has imperfect virtue but leads by means of clear and consistent laws and commands, thus gaining the trust of people at home and allies abroad:

> Although virtue may not be up to the mark, nor were norms fully realized, yet when the principle of all under heaven is somewhat gathered together, punishments and rewards are already trusted by all under heaven, all below the ministers know what to expect. Once administrative commands are made plain, even if one sees one's chances for gain defeated, yet there is no cheating the people; contracts are already sealed, even if one sees one's chances for gain defeated, yet there is no cheating one's partners. If it is so, then the troops will be strong and the town will be firm and enemy states will tremble in fear. Once it is clear the states stand united, your allies will trust you. . . . This is to attain hegemony by establishing strategic reliability. (ch. 11)

The worst kind of state is led by a tyrant devoid of any virtue and who wields the sword as a means to make people afraid at home and abroad. He relies on military power to expand his territory and keeps people in line with harsh laws and punishments. According to Xunzi, "the method based on brute strength will reach an impasse" (ch. 16) and the tyrant is sure to come to a bad end.

In short, the more a ruler relies on informal rituals to generate a sense of community and social trust, the more successful and long-lasting the state and the better off the people. The more a ruler relies on laws and commands to make people afraid and atomized, the more the state will face threats at home and abroad and the more people will suffer. Note, however, that even the most successful state ruled by a humane king cannot entirely do without law. There is an ever-present risk that people will fall prey to the bad tendencies of human nature. Even the sage king needs laws and punishments to deal with such people: "To forget your own person below, to forget your family in the middle, and to forget your lord above—this is something the laws and punishments will not pardon, something the sage king will not accept" (ch. 4). The humane king will do his best to improve people's nature by means of informal rituals, but if that doesn't work, there is a need for laws to punish the reprobates. A contemporary Chinese saying expresses Xunzi's view of the relation between law and ritual: "先礼后兵 *xianli houbing*," literally, "first ritual, then (military) force," but meaning something like: It's best to use informal means such as rituals to establish social peace and generate socially beneficial outcomes, but if that doesn't work, then it's okay to use legally backed punishment as a second (or last) resort.

Now back to the case of drunk driving in China. About fifteen years ago, nobody openly defended the practice. At some level, people knew it was bad. But it was still common to drive after a few drinks. It would have been almost rude not to serve fiery white liquor (白酒 *bai jiu*) to guests in Chinese restaurants;[8] and the stronger the better, with 53 percent alcohol preferred to the measly 38 percent. Drunk drivers would head back home, with predictably disastrous consequences. Alarmed by data that showed that at least 20 percent of serious road crashes were alcohol related, the Chinese government decided to crack down on drunk driving. Educational campaigns meant to change people's selfish habits clearly had no effect. Almost overnight, the authorities set up frequent random sobriety checks. At first, the penalties were not so harsh: Drivers were fined and not permitted to drive for three months. That didn't work much, either. Then punishments were increased to compulsory jail time for first offenders, with zero tolerance of any blood alcohol level and an automatic six-month driving ban, followed by a need to retake a driving course and pass practical and written exams for those who planned to drive again. Fear worked. Eventually, attitudes changed, and drinking and driving became universally frowned on. Death rates caused by drunk drivers plunged nationwide,[9] and random checks, now few and far between, have become almost superfluous. Gone are the days when drivers would feel pressure to drink alcohol in restaurants; when they do drink, sober friends offer to drive them home, and if that's not possible, drunk drivers call the services of paid drivers who wait outside restaurants with tiny bicycles that can be folded into car trunks.

In short, the government tried to tame people's selfish nature by means of education and ritual, and when that didn't work, it tried harsh punishments to enforce norms that people knew, deep down, had social benefits. Eventually, the punishments closed the gap between the norm and the practice and the government could rely mainly on moral self-regulation instead of harsh punishment, but without completely doing away with laws that served as last-resort checks on selfish and dangerous behavior. More or less as Xunzi would have recommended: Best to rely on informal means of regulation that transform people's selfish tendencies, and if that doesn't work, use the strong arm of the law.[10]

I confess these musings are not driven solely by theoretical concerns. Shortly after I arrived in Beijing, I passed a driver's exam that had stern warnings about the need not to drive under the influence. In principle, I agreed with such warnings. In practice, however, I often drove after a few drinks, thinking it wasn't a big deal. Finally, and deservedly, I got caught. It happened one evening about ten years ago when my (then) wife and I invited a journalist from a leading conservative newspaper in the United Kingdom for dinner at a Thai restaurant. We owned the restaurant with some friends and had a private room in the back for such occasions. The conversation flowed freely, with frank political talk about China's present and future. In my pompous moments, I thought of the restaurant as our contribution to civil society in China, similar to Viennese cafés at the beginning of the twentieth century and "existentialist cafés" in mid-century Paris. I didn't do any work for the restaurant, but it felt good when I'd go every Friday afternoon and be greeted as "老板 *laoban*" (boss) by "my" employee/waiter, who would then prepare a super-charged double gin and tonic. I didn't drink much on that particular evening: the usual gin and tonic, followed by a bottle of wine shared three ways over the course of a few hours. When we were done, I offered to drive our journalist friend back to his flat, which he was renting from us. On the way, we were stopped by a policeman who gave me a breathalyzer test. It was the early days of the anti-drunk-driving campaign, and I didn't know about such random checks. I failed the test. Surprised, I got out of the car and asked for another test. How could I fail a test when I had imbibed "only" a (double) gin and tonic and a couple of glasses of wine over the course of three hours? This time, I failed the test with flying colors. The policeman smirked, and I had a feeling that I was doomed. The policeman said that he'd have to take my license away. I pleaded, "Is there any other way?" (有没有别的办法?) and assumed a cute and vulnerable expression. The policeman took my driver's license away. I asked how could I drive home without a license, and he pointed to a nearby driver-worker who could drive my car for a fee. I had to pay a fine of 500 rmb (about U.S.$60) and was barred from driving for three months.

I returned to my car—in the passenger's seat—and told our journalist friend what had happened. He said that he was quite impressed by the rule of law in China. He noticed that a camera had filmed my interaction with the policeman, which limited the possibility of any bribery. He had previously reported from India for a five-year stint, and he said that it's unlikely a foreigner would have been stopped for traffic violations in India (there was still what he called a "white man's privilege"). A few days later, our journalist friend wrote an article in his newspaper detailing the incident to make the surprising point that (sometimes) the rule of law seems more secure in China than in India. The article became widely disseminated among the expatriate community in Beijing and several of my friends wrote to me about it. I was not named, but the article had details that pointed in my direction (how many foreign academics own restaurants in Beijing?). I laughed it off. A week later, however, my wife and I were summoned by my father-in-law to the living room. He was reading *Cankao Xiaoxi*, the official newspaper that translates news about China in foreign newspapers (needless to say, it translates the good news, not the bad news). My father-in-law—a Communist revolutionary who joined the People's Liberation Army as a teenager and fought in the anti-Japanese war, the civil war against the KMT, and the Korean War[11]—read the article out loud and then looked me in the eye. My heart sank, but he said: "You see, there are so many decadent foreigners in Beijing. Never get mixed up with that crowd." I realized that he didn't know the article was about me. My wife had the same realization, and we looked at each other in complicity, keeping silent.

## Back to Shandong

That was about ten years ago. I'm now remarried and leading a more moderate life in the Shandong countryside. No more drunken outings with journalists or alcohol-fueled karaoke. As dean, I'm supposed to be responsible. I did have one relapse, however. One evening, I had dinner with my younger "brother" Professor K. and our graduate students at a village restaurant. It was a typical Shandong banquet, filled with laughter and endless ritualized toasts fueled by 53 percent white liquor. As we stumbled out of the restaurant, I said goodbye to the others and took out the key to my vehicle. Professor K. tried to grab the key out of my hand. I fought back, saying, "It's fine, I'll manage, I'm not going far and I won't run into any police." Professor K., a seventy-sixth-generation descendant of Confucius, scolded me in front of the students. He'd normally appeal to Confucian norms, but he knew that I'd respond with the line about drinking alcohol with no limits. So Professor K. said: "This is a Communist country; we serve other people. Don't be so selfish; you can injure others, not just yourself!" I saluted him, trying to make him laugh, but he was deadly serious. Now I felt terrible. It was a big loss of face in front of my students. How could I be so irresponsible? I came to my senses and handed the key to my senior graduate student. He opened the bicycle lock and walked me back home, along with my two-wheeled vehicle.

# 6

# Teaching Confucianism in China

KONGZI (551–479 BCE)—family name Kong (孔), with "zi" (子) as an honorific title—was a politician, philosopher, and poet. But he is revered first and foremost for his role as a teacher. The saying above the imposing Kongzi statue at the Confucius temple in Qufu is "万世师表," which can be translated as "The Model Teacher for Ten Thousand Generations." Why is Kongzi—known as Confucius in the West—regarded as the teacher of teachers? There are several reasons. He established the earliest form of higher education in China's history and taught students regardless of class or family background. His most famous students were not from privileged families. One of the best-known sayings from the *Analects of Confucius* is "有教无类" (in education, there are no social classes). Kongzi was proud that he "never refused to teach anyone who asked me to, even if they were too poor to offer more than a token offering of a bundle of dried meat for their tuition" (*Analects* 7.7). Kongzi claimed that he was merely transmitting a received tradition (7.1) but he changed the meaning of 君子 (*junzi*) from a noble man with a distinguished family background to an exemplary person with above-average ability and (especially) virtue. Kongzi's position was radical for his day:

He aimed to challenge the idea that family background determines one's fate.[1]

Kongzi did more than argue that students should have equal opportunity to be educated regardless of social background (in his own day, unfortunately, women did not have the opportunity to be educated). He specified the aim of teaching: It involves not just the transmission of knowledge, but, even more important, an effort to train exemplary persons with ability and motivation to work for the public interest. The process of teaching and learning is a life-long relation between teacher and students, based on respect and mutual affection. Kongzi also developed a unique teaching method: He tailored what he taught to the needs of each individual student. When Kongzi was asked why he gave seemingly contradictory answers to the same question—whether one can immediately put into practice what one has learned—posed by two different students, he responded "*Qiu* holds himself back, and so I tried to urge him on. *You* has the energy of two, and so I tried to restrain him" (11.22). Different students need to be improved in different ways, which helps to explain why Kongzi gave so many different responses to questions such as what is 仁 (*ren*) (variously translated as love, humaneness, compassion, benevolence, and authoritative conduct). Those who first read the *Analects of Confucius*—a text compiled by Kongzi's students long after his death—are often puzzled by its seemingly scattered structure and can't understand what's so important about a thin book with cute aphorisms and no unifying argument.[2] But if the text is read as some sort of post-modern (or premodern) play that needs to be pieced together by the reader, with Kongzi in dialogue with different students who have different needs and interests, the text comes to life. For first-time readers, I'd suggest learning about each student before attempting to grapple with the *Analects* so as to better understand why Kongzi said what he said.[3]

If there's one takeaway from Kongzi's teaching method, it's that teaching needs to be intensively focused on the particularity of each student, with lots of give and take between teacher and student. In the West, Confucius has the reputation of a stiff and boring old "master" propounding truths to disciples who blindly take on board the teacher's sayings. But Kongzi didn't think that students can be improved by being treated as an undifferentiated mass who have no opportunity to question the teacher. The teacher can also be wrong. Dialogue is two-way, even though the teacher, by virtue of being a teacher, is usually doing the teaching. For teaching to be effective, the teacher should learn about the unique character of each student, which requires prolonged interaction in different contexts. Practically speaking, it means that the ideal classroom should be small in size, with each individual student given the opportunity to improve in his or her own way and to engage with the teacher both inside and outside of the formal classroom setting.[4]

## Teaching and Drinking

It's no easy task: Kongzi himself is supposed to have had three thousand students, of whom only seventy-two understood and practiced his teachings. His followers can expect a similarly low success rate and I was no exception. I first taught Confucianism in a systematic way at Schwarzman College, an academic joint venture between the United States and China established as part of Tsinghua University in 2016. Before that, I taught political theory at Tsinghua's Department of Philosophy, and I could incorporate some Confucian classics into my courses on political theory, but the teaching of Confucianism was largely the preserve of professors trained in Chinese philosophy, who could teach the classics in Chinese to Chinese students. As a Westerner, I was expected to focus on Western political theory. But Schwarzman College is an English-language program with 80 percent foreign students, so I was offered the opportunity to teach Confucianism in English as part of a course on Chinese political culture, co-taught with Professor W., China's finest intellectual historian. The problem, however, is that our course was one of four core courses (students had to choose three out of four), and nearly every student in the first-year cohort chose our course. How to teach Confucianism to a class of more than one hundred students from diverse academic and cultural backgrounds?

To make it more interesting for the students, we decided to organize the teaching part of the course into a kind of debate between the two professors. My co-teacher had a different orientation—more historical and more skeptical of Confucianism as a guide for the modern world—and we'd repeatedly comment on and criticize each other's ideas during the lecture period. The content of the course itself was organized as a kind of debate: Confucians versus Legalists, Confucians versus Communists, and so on. We could draw on almost unlimited funding from Schwarzman College's large endowment to invite distinguished scholars from abroad for even more diverse teaching perspectives. But how to tailor what we taught to each individual student's interests and weaknesses, as Kongzi would have advised? We divided the class into four groups for the discussion sessions, but each group was still too large—about twenty-five students—to really get to know each student. But we could do more. The Berggruen Institute sponsored two female Confucian scholars from abroad who gave talks in our class and organized smaller (voluntary) discussion groups on the *Analects* for interested students (a clear way to send the message that modern-day Confucianism is not just for men). I organized two (voluntary) small groups to discuss classic texts from the Confucian tradition—one in Chinese and one in English for students who didn't read and speak Chinese well—which allowed for more prolonged interaction with some students. I supervised several theses with Confucian themes and had lengthy discussions with talented students who could be gently pushed to improve in different ways.[5]

What's really distinctive about Schwarzman College is that it provides the possibility for interaction with students outside of the classroom setting. Students—called "scholars," modeled after Rhodes scholars—live at the college, which provides free room and board for the one-year master's degree. Teachers can also stay there, and I spent two months living at the college during my intensive course. I dined with students and learned more about them via informal chitchat. I also partook of festivities with students—the college has its own drinking establishment called the Master Kong Pub—which allowed for more lasting friendships. We could also draw on resources to organize trips outside of Beijing. I took the class for a weekend to Qufu, two hours by fast train from Beijing, to visit the Confucian temple and other Confucian sites. My Kong "brother"—who would join my faculty at Shandong University the following year—served as a tour guide and proudly told the visitors that he'd be buried in the Kong family cemetery. After a day of touring, we had a sumptuous banquet and I made sure that each table had a bottle of fiery 孔府家酒 (Kong Mansion liquor).[6] I organized an informal quiz based on what we had seen that day, with the winning table getting an extra bottle of liquor. Not surprisingly, the drinking quickly got out of hand. I tried to control matters by asking progressively more subjective questions (e.g., What's the most beautiful thing you saw today?) and en-suring that the prize would go to the table with a couple of graduates from the West Point Military Academy, on the as-sumption that they'd be more disciplined.[7] But winning the prize led them to sing the American national anthem, which antagonized some Chinese students. We scattered after the meal, with most students stumbling to a karaoke bar, and I brought a handful of students who spoke good Chinese for another meal and round of drinking with Kong family descen-dants and their local friends. The next day, we organized a soc-cer game against the Kongs and, notwithstanding the hangovers, the Schwarzman scholars managed a one-one tie, a face-saving result for all sides.

In retrospect, the trip to Qufu was both the high and the low point of my experience teaching Confucianism to foreigners. On the one hand, it was a memorable experience for the Schwarzman scholars: They will never forget playing soccer against Kong family descendants in Kongzi's hometown. But word got back about drinking without limits. How about the feelings of Schwarzman scholars who didn't drink alcohol? We did have some practicing Muslim students in our class. And what if some students hurt themselves or committed misdeeds? The Schwarzman program was just getting started and it would take a big reputational hit. The following years, the program became more tightly regulated. Funds were cut off for side trips to Qufu. Restrictions were put in place that barred students and teachers from drinking alcohol together. Our course was down-graded to an optional course and, with less teaching time, the two professors could no longer debate each other.[8] Perhaps I can console myself with the thought that some students vividly experienced Confucianism in action, even if it may not have led to moral improvement.

In any case, I was appointed as dean at Shandong University in January 2017, which provided the opportunity to teach Confucianism to Chinese students. I was appointed mainly because of my scholarly commitment to Confucianism, and I could design my own courses on Confucianism. My academic Chinese had improved and I could teach Chinese students in Chinese. And now I could control student numbers for my graduate classes. I capped the number at twelve students and decided that we'd discuss Xunzi's political thought. Xunzi (c. 310–220 BCE) is, to my mind, the greatest political theorist in the Confucian tradition. He lived during the bloodiest period in Chinese history—the final stages of the Warring States era—but still managed to come up with an original and systematic work that draws insights from other traditions and provides morally informed guidance for public officials in different contexts. Our students would be familiar with the basics of Xunzi's thought and they had all memorized the opening chapter, "An Exhortation to Learning," for the national university entrance examinations (*gaokao*). I decided that we'd read chapters that shed light on the different obligations of different types of public officials—"The Humane King and the Hegemon," "The Way to Be a Lord," and "The Way to Be a Minister"—and go through each chapter carefully, one line at a time.

Here's what I did to ensure that I'd get to know the outlook (if not the character) of each of my students. Before the seminar, I asked students to prepare six questions or comments based on the reading for that week: two on passages they agreed with and why, two on passages they disagreed with and why, and two on passages they didn't quite understand. That way I knew, more or less, how each student reacted to the text and I could structure the discussion according to their interests and puzzlements. I'd pit students with different outlooks against each other (in a polite way, asking student X, You seem to disagree with student Y; why is that?) and let them spell out (if not sort out) their differences. This teaching strategy not only encouraged participation by all, it also clarified the distinctive outlook of each student and I could try to teach each student according to his or her needs and interests. For grading purposes, I asked them to submit a long essay on Xunzi's political thought (generally speaking, the essays were excellent, as good as, if not better than, most essays submitted by students I had taught at the top-ranked Tsinghua University). At the end of the seminar, I brought my students to Lanling in southern Shandong Province to visit Xunzi's memorial grave site. My status as dean at Shandong University helps to arrange meetings with local officials in Shandong, and we were hosted by Lanling cadres. In conversation, they bemoaned the decision to expunge Xunzi from sagehood status in 1530 (more than 450 years after he had been enshrined in 1084), which meant that he had been expelled from Confucian temples. Our hosts provided a grand banquet and I gave a speech exhorting my students to help with official rehabilitation of the great scholar Xunzi.[9] The meal was fueled with Lanling white liquor (白酒) and I could observe how my students acted under the influence of the local "truth serum" (and they could observe the teacher). It's not necessarily a teaching strategy I'd recommend outside of Shandong Province, but the seminar is the closest I'd ever come to Kongzi's teaching ideal.

## Students Gone Rogue

The Confucian teaching ideal is not just to help talented students improve but also to identify students with the potential to surpass the teacher's teachings. As Kongzi put it, "The younger generation should be held in awe: After all, how do we know that those yet to come will not surpass our contemporaries? It's only when one reaches forty or fifty years of age and still has done nothing of note that we should withdraw our sense of awe" (9.23). If Confucianism is a quest for never-ending self-improvement, it should mean that the tradition improves over time, helped by students who learn from teachers and push the teachings in new and better directions. That's the theory, anyway. Off the top of my head, it's hard to think of any student who surpassed a great thinker in the Confucian tradition (Kongzi's favorite student, Yan Hui, died at the tragically young age of thirty-two, before he could develop and practice his ideas for posterity). But it's easy to think of students who did the opposite: Instead of building on the teacher's teaching, they tried to destroy it. The most famous case is Xunzi's student Han Feizi, who took on board his teacher's assumption that humans have a tendency to badness but rejected the possibility that they can be improved. Instead of a society governed first and foremost by informal rituals, as Xunzi advocated, Han Feizi argued for a quasi-totalitarian state ruled by harsh laws. The aim is to strengthen the state rather than benefit the people, and Confucian troublemakers (like his teacher Xunzi) who cast doubt on this political project should be put to death.[10] In the Western tradition, a (fictitious) equivalent might be a student of Hobbes who extends the idea of the Leviathan state in even more terrifying directions without mentioning that the ultimate moral purpose of the whole thing is to protect the right to life. We can argue about the extent to which teachers bear responsibility for students gone rogue, but the fact that Xunzi spawned students such as Han Feizi blackened his reputation and helps to explain why he was expunged from the Confucian canon and has yet to fully recover, more than twenty-two centuries later.

Why would students want to turn against their teachers? It might have to do with the heavy expectations placed on the teacher in the Confucian tradition. The teacher is supposed not just to educate the student but also to serve as a moral role model. If the teacher disappoints the student, the student may lash out at the teacher. But perhaps it's something deeper. In the Confucian tradition, the best teacher is a father-like figure who both educates and showers the student with love and care. As Freud reminds us, however, such emotions can lead to less-than-healthy unconscious desires on the part of the recipient. I had my own experience with what we might call an Oedipal student, but I won't recount the story here. It's too upsetting.

# 7

# The Communist Comeback

IN 2008, I published a book proclaiming the end of Marxist ideology in China.[1] Marxism was dead as a motivating value system. Few serious thinkers in China openly defended Marxism as a guiding ideology for the modern world. The Chinese Communist Party seemed to be communist in name only, and it increasingly emphasized "Chinese characteristics," meaning commitment to pragmatic change and to China's own cultural traditions such as Confucianism. I predicted that the CCP would soon be renamed the Chinese Confucian Party.

Ironically, the Marxist tradition mounted its comeback at the same time, in both official and unofficial circles. It started after the 2007–2008 global financial crisis, when Chinese scholars began to look to Marx's critique of capitalism to understand what went wrong with market societies. Since 2012, President Xi has reaffirmed the Marxist essence of the CCP and used harsh means to rein in the excesses of capitalism. Under the banner of "common prosperity," the government has mounted efforts to eliminate absolute poverty and reduce the polarization between rich and poor. The ideal is similar to Marx's ideal of lower communism: "From each according to his ability, to each according to his contribution,"[2] meaning that hard work will be rewarded and workers won't be penalized due to unequal social and economic opportunities. The goal is not equal distribution of income (or distribution according to need, as in higher communism), but rather to equalize starting points so that all citizens have equal opportunities to be rewarded for hard work.[3] The means employed include anti-monopoly measures against Big Tech, an attempt to deflate the real estate bubble, and crackdowns on private businesses that offered online and offline tutoring classes to those who could afford them. Defenders of the free market worry that such measures will dampen the entrepreneurial spirit that drives China's economic dynamism.[4] But the government seems prepared to take the risk. Whatever one thinks about the means employed to realize "common prosperity," it's hard to doubt the government's commitment to communism. To use Confucian language, the Chinese Communist Party has "rectified" its name, meaning that the party's conduct now more closely corresponds to its name's true significance.[5]

The more explicit commitment to communism is also evident in academia. A few years ago, I almost felt sorry for scholars of Marxism in China because they were often viewed as second-rate thinkers who lacked the talent to do serious scholarly work. Today, many promising scholars go to the School of Marxism, where they are showered with resources. The same goes for students. In the 1980s, academically gifted students rarely tried to join the party: They were not committed to Marxism and sought to develop their talents outside of the party structure. Today, top students compete ferociously to join the party, and applicants for academic jobs who are party members proudly mention their affiliation on their résumés. My own faculty has a School of Scientific Socialism that was viewed, until recently, as a somewhat embarrassing relic from the past.

All other universities in China had abolished such departments in the age of reform, but we failed to do so because our faculty's founding father, Professor Z., was committed to its existence.[6] Today, we proudly mention that we are the only university in China with a School of Scientific Socialism and our students pursue graduate work in China's leading universities. In my second year as dean, I joined a university-level annual meeting with other deans and leading university administrators to summarize our faculty's achievements. I didn't know how to proceed at first because all the other leaders started by proclaiming their commitment to the party's leadership and the socialist vision. A few years ago, I would have dismissed such "propaganda" and never dreamed I'd be in a position where I had to say something similar. But here I was. So I said, half-jokingly, I'm not yet a party member but I support the communist ideal. To my surprise, there was laughter accompanied by sustained and sincere applause, and I was specifically commended for that part of the speech.

Western observers often attribute the revival of communism to President Xi's personal commitments: As the *New York Times* put it, he seeks to "remake the Communist Party history in his image."[7] Without Xi, in other words, China could have continued along the road of market-based economic reforms and perhaps implemented democratic political reforms. From a Marxist perspective, however, it could be argued that President Xi is faithfully following the imperatives of Karl Marx's theory of history. China, as Deng Xiaoping recognized, had to go through a capitalist phase to develop the productive forces on the way to communism, but now is the time to transition to communism.

In Marx's view, the capitalist mode of production treats workers as mere tools in the productive process and puts technology to use for the purpose of enriching a small minority of capitalists.[8] But Marx recognized that capitalism has an important virtue: It has the consequence of developing the productive forces—technology and the knowledge to make use of it—more than any previous economic system. The reason is that capitalists compete with one another to make a profit; hence they have an incentive to develop ever more efficient means to produce goods, creating a large material surplus without which communism would not be feasible.

In the Marxist framework, the moral point of the whole ugly process is to free the large mass of humankind from the need to engage in drudge labor. Technology will be highly developed, and at a certain point—the moment of revolution—private property will be abolished and machines will be made to do the work for the betterment of humanity instead of the interests of one small class. Technology will do the dirty work needed to meet people's physical needs, and people will finally be free to go fishing, read books, and create works of beauty.

This Marxist interpretation of China's history is not a fanciful reconstruction of the past. Deng's dictum was that the party would "let some people get rich first." But the rest of the people were meant to get rich later, with the party leading the process. The CCP's constitution specifies that "the realization of communism is the highest ideal and ultimate goal of the Party."[9] The party never let go of the ultimate levers of economic power: The "private" ownership of homes in China is limited to a seventy-year lease, with the implication that private property can (and should) be expropriated at some point in the future, if required to bring about a truly equal communist society. The commitment to "higher communism" informed the work of Wang Huning, China's most influential political theorist—adviser to Presidents Jiang Zemin and Hu Jintao, and now a member of the ruling Standing Committee of the Politburo.[10] President Xi himself invoked Marx's theory of history: "Marxism argues that humankind will inevitably take a path to communism, but it will be achieved through historical phases. Comrade Deng Xiaoping said socialism is the primary stage of communism and China is at the primary stage of socialism, in other words, at the undeveloped stage. With that judgment, he promoted reform and opening-up, made historic achievements and ushered in a new era. We already have a rich material basis for realizing new, even higher goals."[11]

In Marxist terms, China seems to be transitioning to the "dictatorship of the proletariat," the political superstructure of "lower communism." Marx argued that countries need to go through a "dictatorship of the proletariat" in between the capitalist and higher communist phases of history. Dictatorship is necessary to put down the "remnants of the bourgeoisie" and to ensure that people are trained in both practical and theoretical skills, thus allowing for the flourishing of the "fully developed individual" in communist society. But the dictatorship is short-term. Marx predicted that the state would eventually "wither away" in higher communism: Developed machinery would produce all the goods human beings need, we'd all be truly free and equal with the opportunity to develop our many-sided talents as we see fit, resources would be distributed according to need, and there would be no need for a coercive state to protect the interests of a ruling class (since there would be no ruling class). The end of history, in Marx's view, is an anarchist society where order can be secured without any coercion.[12]

## The Dictatorship of the Bureaucracy

The nineteenth-century anarchist thinker Mikhail Bakunin identified a deep problem with Karl Marx's theory of history. Bakunin endorsed Marx's critique of capitalism as well as his ideal of a classless society without a state, but he strongly objected to the dictatorship of the proletariat: "If you took the most ardent revolutionary, vested him in absolute power, within a year he would be worse than the Tsar himself."[13] Instead of a transitional phase between the abolition of capitalism and the establishment of a classless communist society, the former proletarians would seize power and become a dictatorial ruling class that fiercely resists challenges to its power. The ruling class would entrench itself as a self-interested bureaucracy that serves itself rather than the people: They will "look down on the whole common workers' world from the height of the state. They will no longer represent the people, but themselves and their pretensions to people's government. Anyone who can doubt this knows nothing of the nature of men." Marx acknowledged Bakunin's critique and copied his response in a notebook: "If Mr. Bakunin only knew something about the position of a manager in a workers' cooperative factory, all his dreams of domination would go the devil." Let's grant Marx's assumption that workers' cooperative factories can be made to work effectively with proletarian-managers freed of the drive for power. But how would a large-scale society select benevolent proletarian dictators and how are those dictators supposed to eventually guide themselves out of power? Bakunin asked, "Will the entire proletariat perhaps stand at the end of the government? . . . The Germans number around forty million. Will, for example, all forty million be members of the government?" Marx replied: "Certainly! The whole thing begins with the self-government of the commune." And elections, if necessary, will not have a political character: "Election is a political form present in the smallest Russian commune and artel. The character of the election does not depend on this name, but on the economic foundation, the economic situation of the voters, and as soon as the functions ceased to be political ones, there exists 1) no government function, 2) the distribution of the general functions has become a business matter, that gives no one domination, 3) election has nothing of its present political character."[14] Marx does not specify how such non-political elections designed to select leaders who do not dominate anyone are supposed to work.

Not surprisingly, there is no support in subsequent history for Marx's idea that the "dictatorship of the proletariat" is workable in the short term and dispensable in the long term. As Bakunin predicted, when revolutionaries take over the state, they become a new ruling class. The CCP has changed the terminology of post-capitalist society from the "dictatorship of the proletariat" to the "primary stage of socialism." But the problem remains the same: How is the political ruling class supposed to guide itself out of power once the country becomes wealthy to the point that nobody needs to work for a living and everyone is free to develop their creative talents? David Stasavage argues that China's two-millennia-long history of complex bureaucracy reduces the likelihood of a transition to democracy.[15] Given China's dominant political culture, the transition to communist anarchy is even less likely. Not to mention that bureaucratic rule has become even more entrenched in the period of reform. The need for bureaucracy and rule by experts becomes even more pressing as countries become economically complex and socially diverse. So it's not surprising that China has reestablished a strong form of bureaucratic rule since the period of economic reform in the late 1970s, with administrators increasingly selected according to level of education and by means of ultra-competitive examinations and performance evaluations at lower levels of government. Today, China has the most complex and intrusive bureaucracy the world has ever seen, and with each passing day it's harder than ever to imagine the "withering away of the state." On the contrary: There are legitimate fears that the CCP harnesses big data and artificial intelligence (AI) to monitor social critics and "to perfect the police state."[16]

But let's assume that the CCP is truly committed to higher communism as the final end goal and eventually aims to get there via more humane means and less repression. Even if Chinese bureaucrats somehow agree on the need to disband as China approaches the conditions for "higher communism," we need to ask what will happen to China's security state so long as other large powers such as the United States maintain capitalist relations of production and a form of government that is hostile to communism. As Marx recognized, higher communism must be global to be successful: "Empirically, communism is only possible as the act of the dominant peoples 'all at once' and simultaneously, which presupposes the universal development of productive forces and the world intercourse bound up with communism."[17] Empirically, communism seems to be impossible.

Perhaps we need a bit more imagination. Over the past few years, the ideal of higher communism has been revived as a topic of theoretical interest among political thinkers in China.[18] The main reason is that AI can provide the material conditions for realization of the ideal. In the short to medium term, AI may put millions of workers out of work and exacerbate inequality. In the long term, however, it should be possible to put AI to work for the benefit of humanity. Intelligent advanced machines would do the boring and mind-dulling work that produces the goods and services necessary for human well-being, and humans would be free to realize their creative essences through meaningful and mind-expanding labor. Marx himself foresaw the possibility of advanced machinery replacing the drudge work of laborers.[19] But technological optimism needs to be tempered by the possibility that things can go wrong.

Marx didn't foresee the possibility that intelligent machines might eventually outsmart even "fully developed individuals," with the risk that human beings could be enslaved by machine-masters. As Nick Bostrom argues, superintelligence can develop to the point that it poses an existential threat to humanity.[20] Given the possibility of malevolent AI, it would be foolhardy to even hope that the state will wither away. A strong state will always be necessary to ensure that AI does not invert the human-machine hierarchy with humans on top and machines at the bottom, or at least to prolong our dominance as long as possible.[21]

Even if it's all good news on the AI front, it's hard to imagine the withering away of the state. Dealing with pandemics and climate change may require a strong and effective state.[22] I certainly hope we can abolish nuclear weapons, but meanwhile we need to regulate them and regulations need some teeth. There will always be some scarce resources that need to be distributed in a fair way, and, contra Marx, it's not likely that such "business" matters can be decided in a non-politicized way without the backup of coercive laws. David Chalmers envisages a future where we spend most of our lives in virtual reality, so we can all afford to live in seafront villas because the cost of digital goods is marginal.[23] But who would get that thirty-year-old bottle of *mao tai* (茅台)? Given the choice, I somehow doubt my alcohol-loving friends in Shandong would settle for a digital form of exclusive liquor.

## Toward Confucian Communism

In short, the state will not, and should not, wither away. Let's stop dreaming that Chinese bureaucrats will eventually decide to make themselves superfluous. The right question is how to increase the likelihood that public officials will effectively serve the public interest and how to decrease the likelihood that public resources will be misappropriated for private interests. Here, the Marxist tradition has almost nothing to offer (and neither does the liberal tradition).[24] But the Confucian tradition has rich resources. Confucian scholars, regardless of their differences, have always recognized the need for public officials with above-average ability and virtue, and they argued about appropriate means of training such officials and limiting their power. The Confucian political ideal of "the Great Unity" in the classic Han Dynasty *Book of Rituals* sounds vaguely communist—people love their own families and the public at large, the elderly and the needy are taken care of, adults use their abilities to the fullest, resources are relatively plentiful, and selfish thoughts are dismissed—and it inspired Mao Zedong two millennia later. But even such political utopias emphasize the need to select public officials with superior ability and virtue (选贤与能).[25] So, it's no coincidence that official Communist Party schools in China such as the Academy for the Education of Virtuous Public Officials (政德教育学院) in Qufu increasingly teach the Confucian classics to public officials as part of an effort to reduce corruption and inculcate a public-spirited work ethic.

My conclusion is that China's political future is likely to be shaped by both Communism and Confucianism. So, should the Chinese Communist Party change its name? In typical Chinese pragmatic fashion, the solution may be to add another name, just as the "School of Central Socialism" (中央社会主义学院) in Beijing added the name "Chinese Culture Institute" (中华文化学院) in 1997 to reflect its increased focus on the promotion of Chinese culture. The institute uses different names in different contexts and the same could be true of the CCP. Given that "communism" is such a bogey word in the West (especially the United States), perhaps the CCP can call itself the Chinese Confucian Party when it deals with Westerners and stick to the Chinese Communist Party at home.

# 8

# Censorship, Formal and Informal

JOHN STUART MILL's *On Liberty*, first published in 1859, is the most influential defense of free speech ever written. What is less well known is that Mill worried more about "public opinion" than about state censorship. As Mill puts it, the tyranny of public opinion is "more formidable than many kinds of political oppression, since, though not usually upheld by such extreme penalties, it leaves fewer means of escape, penetrating much more deeply into the details of life, and enslaving the soul itself."[1] Yes, he was writing in Victorian England and our time may not be as conformist. But it's worth asking if his worries are still relevant today. My own experience writing about Chinese politics suggests that it depends on the context. Today, Mill's thesis is right about the West but wrong about China.

In China, it will come as no great surprise that the heavy hand of state censorship is the biggest problem. And things have gotten worse the past few years. In 2015, Education Minister Yuan Guiren called for the strengthening of Marxist ideology in universities and a ban on "teaching materials that disseminate Western values in our classrooms."[2] On the face of it, such regulations are absurd. It would mean banning not just the ideas of

John Stuart Mill and John Rawls but also those of thinkers such as Karl Marx and Friedrich Engels.

Pronouncements against the influence of Western values contradict what's really happening in higher education in China. There have been recurrent campaigns against foreign interference since the 1980s, and yet the trend has been consistent: more international links with Western universities, more academic meritocracy and less political ideology in the selection and promotion of professors, and experimentation with different modes of liberal arts education. In my faculty, an academic committee selects and promotes professors based on academic merit, and political considerations rarely intervene.[3] Of course, the government could reverse these trends, but the nation's leaders know full well that a modern educational system needs to learn as much as it can from abroad.

In my case, I've been teaching political theory in mainland China for two decades—thirteen years at Tsinghua University, then six years at Shandong University—and I continue to be pleasantly surprised by the amount of freedom in the classroom.[4] I recognize that the classics are less subject to censorship than works in contemporary political science and theory. I also recognize that English-language books are not censored as heavily as works in Chinese.[5] Still, I routinely discuss politically sensitive topics, and much of what I teach would fall in the "prohibited" category if official warnings were enforced to the letter. At Shandong University, I've been teaching an advanced undergraduate course in political philosophy. Here is what I say in the syllabus:

This course is a basic introduction to the main principles of political philosophy. The history of political philosophy, whether in China or the West, is a history of debates about contrasting political values: What matters more, freedom or community? Equality or hierarchy? Democracy or political meritocracy? Nationalism or cosmopolitanism? Different thinkers in China and the West have put forward different arguments for prioritizing different values, depending on their political ideals and visions of the good life. These political values recur in different times and places and they are still being debated today. In this course, we will discuss some of the more influential arguments for and against these contrasting political values in the history of political thought.

My course has been made into a bilingual MOOC (I use English to discuss Western thinkers and Chinese to discuss Chinese thinkers and I assign works in both languages).[6] In class, students say what's on their minds, as they would in any Western university. I try to present the ideas of great political theorists in the best possible light, and let students debate their merits among themselves.[7] If it's a class on Mill's *On Liberty*, I'll try to make the best possible case for freedom of speech, and in a class on Confucius's *Analects*, I'll do the same for the value of harmony. I invite leading thinkers from China and the West to give guest lectures, whatever their political outlooks. At Tsinghua, I invited the leading British liberal thinker Timothy Garton Ash to deliver a lecture on Mill's defense of free speech. The good news is that my classrooms have been almost completely free from political interference. The one exception happened shortly after I arrived in Beijing in 2004. I wanted to teach a course on Marxism but was told that it would not be advisable because my interpretation might differ from official ideology. Human rights and democracy are fine to teach, but not Marxism. I learned to get around that constraint by teaching the material without putting the word "Marxist" in the course title.[8]

Research is more challenging. In my faculty, younger professors complain that they face increasing constraints publishing works in Chinese: Research on, say, social protests or workers' rights that would have passed the censors a few years ago can no longer be published in Chinese-language political science periodicals.[9] What was once a sophisticated form of censorship of works in Chinese has become increasingly crude, with whole books banned because of a few "sensitive" parts.[10] For those of us writing in English, the censors do not interfere, but they spring into action when works are translated in Chinese. The Chinese translation of my book *China's New Confucianism* was due to be published in 2008, but I was told that it couldn't go to press because of the Olympics: Nothing remotely critical about contemporary politics in China could be published when the whole world was watching the country. In 2009, the sixtieth anniversary of the founding of modern China made it another "sensitive" year. In early 2010, the upcoming World Expo in Shanghai provided an excuse for delay. To my surprise, my book was finally published during a brief period of a politically "not-so-sensitive" time in the autumn of 2010.

Lately, the censorship regime has intensified. This time, the main reason is President Xi Jinping's anti-corruption campaign, which produces real enemies with a strong motivation to undermine the current leadership.[11] Hence, even more curbs than usual on political publications, no matter how academic. I've ordered books on Amazon that have been confiscated at the border. I've long needed a virtual private network to access the *New York Times* and Google Scholar, but censors have been disrupting the use of VPNs. My tech-savvy students help me to get around the restrictions, but it's a cat-and-mouse game and the cat is getting smarter. My mood varies almost directly with the ease of Internet access, and lately I've often been in a foul mood.

Ironically, I had a particularly hard time accessing sources for my book *The China Model*, which is a largely positive account of the principles underlying the Chinese political system. I had to leave the country for several months to access works on the Internet and banned books in English and Chinese necessary to make my case. The book was eventually accepted for translation, but my heart sank when the editor showed me a thick booklet with corrections demanded by the censors. She said that it's the largest booklet she had ever seen. With great patience and some strategic thinking, we managed to restore about 90 percent of the cuts. To illustrate a point, for example, we referred to an official government source rather than an article in the *Wall Street Journal*. Or sometimes things had to be phrased in a more indirect way. To illustrate the argument that leaders in times of war do not necessarily have the qualities that make them good leaders in times of peace, I replaced "Mao" with "an Asian leader in the twentieth century" on the assumption that the Chinese reader would get the point.[12] What could not be massaged, however, is the suggestion at the end of the book that the Chinese Communist Party change its name to the "Union of Democratic Meritocrats" (民主贤能联盟 *minzhu xianneng lianmeng*) so that the name better reflects the ideals of the ruling organization. The ending of the book was simply cut. My latest book, *Just Hierarchy*, co-authored with Wang Pei, was translated into Chinese and we encountered more politically induced delays: The book could not be published because of the hundredth anniversary of the CCP celebrations in July 2021 and the Winter Olympics in February 2022. We managed to find an opening for publication in May 2022, before the Twentieth Party Congress scheduled for October 2022. But here, too, much of the content was censored, starting with our proposal for a subtitle. (We had proposed "A Progressive Conservative

Perspective" as a subtitle but we were told that the words "pro-gressive" [进步] and "conservative" [保守] are both too politi-cally sensitive to be in the title.)

It's worth asking why I continue to work in an academic en-vironment with such constraints. Half of my family is Chinese, and I have special affection for the country. It helps to have great students and colleagues. In his famous "end of history" article, Francis Fukuyama put his finger on another key reason: A world where nobody argues about political ideals may be peaceful, but it's boring.[13] China is not boring. Chinese-style democratic meritocracy—an ideal that (highly imperfectly) in-forms the political reality—is the only viable alternative to lib-eral democracy in the modern world, and I have a front-row seat for China's experiment. What else could a political theorist ask for? That said, a political theorist—no matter what kind—needs the freedom of speech to communicate his or her ideas.

Actually, I'm not a free-speech fundamentalist. As noted, I made and okayed revisions so that my books would get through the political censors. I'm perfectly willing to rewrite an argument in a somewhat roundabout or indirect way if that's what it takes for my writings to see the light of day. I'm even willing to cut an argument or an example if it's not central to the main thesis. Still, the current trends in China—more repression, less freedom of speech—are deeply worrisome for anybody who cares about free speech in universities. And my views are widely shared in Chinese academia: Whatever people say in public, I haven't met a single Chinese intellectual—socialist, liberal, or Confucian—who argues in private for censorship of scholarly works. Censor-ship only serves to alienate intellectuals. My own students usu-ally say that political reform should take place on the basis of the current political system, not against it. But the more they are prevented from discussing such views, the more disenchanted they will become, and that spells trouble for the long term. Openness, in my view, can only benefit the system.

Are there reasons to be optimistic for the long term? Yes, I think so. The first reason is the change of generational guard. The publishers and editors in China, especially the younger ones, are on the side of academics and want their books to be published. But they must get approval from party *apparatchiks*, elderly revolutionary comrades who may not share modern ideas about the importance of free intellectual exchange. Why are they given power to make decisions? I'd argue that the traditional value of respect for the elderly still plays an important role. This makes me optimistic about the future: Things should improve once the relatively open-minded new generation of leaders occupies more positions of power. That might take a couple of decades, though *glasnost*-like signals from the top would help to speed things up. That said, the youngest generation may be more nationalistic than those who came of age in the 1980s, when Chinese students and intellectuals looked to the West as the standard for social and political progress: My students increasingly look to China's own traditions for inspiration, and they are generally proud of their country's achievements in the past few decades. But that's a good reason for *less* censorship: Today, the younger generation, with more experience abroad and more self-confidence, won't be influenced so readily by "propaganda" from abroad and can be relied on to defend China from unfair criticism. On the other hand, the more people are censored, the more they will direct their ire at their own government.

A second reason for optimism is that it's not just academics and younger publishers and editors who value freedom of speech. Journalists and artists have also felt frustrated by increasing constraints. As Wang Pei and I argued in a comment published in the *South China Morning Post*,[14] the rest of society finally began to notice the dangers of increased censorship when in December 2019, Dr. Li Wenliang alerted colleagues—mainly doctors at high risk of infection—to a new virus that became known as Covid, only to be warned by local authorities not to spread rumors. In February 2020, Dr. Li succumbed to the same virus and died, generating widespread outrage on social media. Dr. Li's fate galvanized public opinion in a new and forceful way, and it looked as though there would be almost overwhelming social pressure for more freedom of speech in the future. The government, we argued, needs to adapt: At the very least, it should think twice before censoring experts who disseminate their research and express worries to their colleagues. It's in the government's own interest to respond to calls for more freedom of speech. As it stands, political leaders are blamed for everything in China because only officially approved views are publicly expressed. With more openness, responsibility will be more diffuse and the government can help to fix things and deal with them efficiently before they explode. And if they do explode, it's often not the fault of central-level leaders, so public inquiries advised by experts can help shift the blame to the local authorities who did wrong.

Political reality has a way of puncturing wishful thinking. I regret to report that things have only tightened up since the death of Dr. Li Wenliang. In 2015, I wrote a comment in the *New York Times* on the prospects for free speech in China with these concluding sentences: "I am confident that things will loosen up eventually. I confess, however, I was even more confident 10 years ago."[15] It's even harder to be optimistic now. But who knows, we might still be pleasantly surprised. I left Singapore in 1994 just as it was getting more repressive, with growing constraints on the freedom of speech. I couldn't even teach Mill's *On*

*Liberty* in class: The head of the department, a member of parlia-ment for the ruling People's Action Party, told me that it was too politically sensitive for undergraduates. At the time, Singapore's universities were far more repressive than those in China. Unex-pectedly, however, Singapore's universities made tremendous progress in terms of the freedom of speech that underpins aca-demic meritocracy. In 2013, I returned to the same department at the National University of Singapore that had fired me two decades earlier so I'd have unconstrained access to materials in English and Chinese that would allow me to write a book on Chinese politics. What a breath of fresh air compared to China! Perhaps Singapore's progress shows the way for China's universi-ties in the not-too-distant future. Might we look back one day at China's current clampdown on freedom of speech as the tail end of a repressive political environment?[16] If it happens in my life-time, I will offer a free glass of *bai jiu* (white liquor) to anyone who reminds me of this promise.

## From Public Intellectual to Minor Bureaucrat

In Western countries, there is no formal system of state cen-sorship. The real threat to the freedom of speech, as J. S. Mill argued, comes from public opinion. Certain public prejudices make some stories more newsworthy than others, and those stories further reinforce those prejudices. It's especially clear in the case of writing about Chinese politics: The public in West-ern countries thinks it's all bad news, and it's hard to publish anything that says otherwise. In 2008, I wrote a comment in the *Guardian* complaining about "the way that China is demonized in the Western press. . . . Anything positive about China leads to accusations about being an 'apologist' for the regime. Once in a while, a story that attempts to provide some context or balance gets placed in the Western press, but they are drowned out by the daily drumbeat of hostile reports."[17]

Looking back, I wonder why I complained so much. Those were the golden days for those of us who wanted to communicate a more nuanced picture of China, including the good news. In my own case, I could publish (what I consider to be) balanced comments about Chinese politics just about anywhere. I was still a relative newcomer in mainland China—I had arrived in 2004—but I had almost open access to leading media outlets in the West. Not to be too pompous, but I could credibly claim to be a public intellectual of global influence. The *Guardian* asked me to write about Chinese society and politics for its newly established "Comment Is Free" online commentary. An op-ed editor from the *New York Times* regularly visited me in Beijing and published almost everything I sent him. I recommended Chinese scholars to write op-eds for the *New York Times* and he floated the possibility of a more formal relationship with mainland Chinese universities. *New York Times* reporters asked for my views about Chinese politics. *Newsweek* asked me to write a guest blog during the 2008 Olympics in Beijing. I published several op-eds in right-leaning publications such as the *Financial Times* and the *Wall Street Journal* as well as longer comments in liberal outlets such as the *Atlantic* and socialist periodicals such as *Dissent*. I was invited to give talks at World Economic Forum annual events in Davos and Dalian as well as smaller WEF events around the world. The editor of *Foreign Affairs* wrote to me saying that he'd like to publish my work in the future. Reporters for Canada's leading newspaper, the *Globe and Mail*, twice wrote profiles of my work in China. I was frequently interviewed on CNN and the BBC. The Canadian Broadcasting Network and the Voice of America filmed long segments about my life in China. I was interviewed in

French by leading media outlets in the Francophone world and my comments were translated into dozens of languages by *Project Syndicate*. Reporters from around the world asked about my book *China's New Confucianism*, which led with an essay titled "From Communism to Confucianism" and predicted that the CCP would be renamed the Chinese Confucian Party.[18] I took pride in hosting salons and connecting foreign journalists and local scholars for informal political discussions at Purple Haze, a restaurant I co-owned in Beijing, and I could see the results of those events in articles and comments published shortly thereafter. I was asked to apply for teaching posts at leading universities in the United States and Canada. There seemed to be genuine curiosity about the experience of a foreign political theorist living and working in Beijing, and I felt that I was at the center of the action.

It all came crashing down. One by one, I lost access to leading media outlets in the West. I'm no longer contacted by any journalists from the Western media. Ironically, the longer I've stayed in China—it has now been nearly two decades—and the more I understand the nuances of society and the political system, the less it has been possible to communicate my views in leading media outlets in the West. What happened? Partly, it's the result of political forces that turned public opinion in the West against China. The demonization of China has exploded to a point I could barely imagine in 2008. In those days, I worried about extreme right-wing militarists in the United States who planned for a long-term confrontation with China. Today all leading voices in the West agree on the "China threat."[19] There is almost universal consensus in the West that China is led by an evil government that is bad to its own people and dangerous to people in other countries. It's extremely difficult to publish views that argue otherwise. Public opinion won't stand for it. In theory, liberals and conservatives in the West agree on the need for an open media environment with diverse and controversial voices that question the *status quo*. In practice, it's almost all one way—bad news—when it comes to China, especially its political system.

Why the change since 2008? Partly, it's the result of more repression in China. Today, it's not just Tibetans who are subject to repression: The Uyghurs, arguably, are subject to even worse repression. Term limits for the president have been abolished, leaving open the possibility of a return to Maoist-style personal dictatorship. In 2013, the Chinese government blocked web access to the *New York Times*, setting the stage for blocking other Western media outlets; not surprisingly, reporting on China soured thereafter. But again, it's not all bad news in China. Today, environmental concerns are taken much more seriously, extreme poverty has been abolished, corruption has been drastically curtailed, and the Chinese government, after the initial debacle in Wuhan, more or less successfully contained Covid until Shanghai was hit by Omicron two years later. Not to mention that China hasn't gone to war since 1979. So why the increased hostility in the West? In my view, the demonization of China, especially of its political system, has gone from bad to worse because of the realization that "they" won't be like "us."[20] This reaction is grounded in a form of self-love. It was perfectly fine to support China's economic and political development so long as "they" were viewed as a somewhat inferior civilization that would eventually learn the truth about the superiority of Western-style capitalism and liberal democracy. But those hopes have faded. For one thing, China has (re) discovered its own past. For most of the twentieth century, Chinese liberals and Marxists looked to the West for inspiration. It may have been flattering for Westerners—look, they want to be just like us!—but there is less sympathy now that Chinese are taking pride their own heritage and turning to their own traditions, such as Confucianism, for thinking about economic, social, and political reform.

The real worry, however, is that "they" will surpass "us." The flaws of Western-style democracy are becoming increasingly evident. Populist leaders with no political experience can get elected by lying on a daily basis and appealing to the people's worst emotions. The United States, in particular, is losing its economic dominance. Whereas once China was denounced for churning out uncreative copycats, today companies such as Huawei are feared because they are more innovative than American competitors. Not to mention that the United States almost completely abandoned its global responsibilities under President Trump (things have improved slightly under President Biden, but national selfishness still dominates on issues like vaccine distribution). Partly, the problems are rooted in the democratic system itself. Global challenges like climate change require concern for future generations in the whole world. But political equality in electoral democracies ends at the boundaries of the political community: Those outside the community are neglected, especially if their interests conflict with those of the voting community. The national, this-generational focus of the democratically elected leaders is part of the system, so to speak: They are meant to serve the community of voters, not future generations, and even less foreigners living outside the political community. Even democracies that work well tend to focus on the interests of citizens and neglect the interests of foreigners and future generations. But political leaders, especially of big countries like China and the United States, make decisions that affect future generations and the rest of the world and they need to consider their interests when they make decisions. Nobody, unfortunately, formally represents the interests of future generations and foreigners in democratic systems.

The Chinese political system, whatever its flaws, does allow for more serious consideration of the needs of future generations and foreigners, and it's not surprising that some analysts expect the country to take the lead in dealing with climate change.[21] Global challenges also require long-term planning. Consider the development of AI: Nobody can predict the future in any detail, but we can be sure that AI will radically upend the way we lead our lives in a few decades' time. Hence, the Chinese government has been developing and implementing strategies for putting AI to socially desirable uses in the future.[22] China's leaders are also aware that China cannot thrive unless its neighbors also thrive: The Belt and Road initiative is meant to support infrastructure in surrounding countries that will provide the foundation for economic development. Large Chinese state-owned enterprises are prepared to take short-term losses for the sake of long-term gains. Political leaders in the United States and other electoral democracies, meanwhile, tend to worry about the next election, and find it difficult to plan beyond four or five years.[23]

What can be done to reduce demonization of the CCP? First, there is a need to break out of the democracy/authoritarian political dichotomy. Packaging the debate in terms of "democracy" versus "autocracy" is not helpful for understanding China's political system. It is wrong to think that all countries that do not use democratic elections to select leaders share the same authoritarian nature. China is not run by a family or by the military. In principle, it is a political meritocracy, meaning equality of opportunity in education and government, with positions of leadership being distributed to relatively virtuous and qualified members of the political community.[24] The idea here is that everybody has the potential to become an exemplary person, but in real life, the capacity to make competent and morally justifiable political judgments varies between people and an important task of the political system is to identify those with above-average capacity. Hence, over the past few decades, China has been building up a complex bureaucratic system that is designed to select and promote public officials with political experience and above-average ability and virtue. Of course, there is a huge gap between the ideal and the reality. China is a highly imperfect political meritocracy, just as the United States is a highly imperfect democracy. But political meritocracy can and should serve as the moral standard for improving the selection of top leaders in China, just as electoral democracy can and should serve as the moral standard for improvement in the United States. The point here is not to deny the validity of universal political values. All countries need to respect basic human rights—"negative rights" not to be killed, tortured, enslaved, as well as "positive rights" to a decent level of material well-being—but we do need to allow for diverse ways of selecting and promoting political leaders. Why should all countries use the same mechanisms to select leaders? Surely, what's appropriate depends on the history, culture, size, and current needs of a country. What works in the United States won't necessarily work in China. Few Chinese intellectuals and political reformers in China would dispute this point, but in the United States and other Western countries, it seems almost impossible to shake dogmatic attachment to the idea that one person, one vote is the only morally legitimate way of selecting political leaders.

As I write these words, I'm aware of what many Western readers will be thinking: This guy has "gone native." He is an apologist, a Communist sympathizer, a fellow traveler, a useful idiot, or, my personal favorite (because it made me laugh), an "academic *wumao*."[25] And that also helps to explain why I've lost access to mainstream media in the West. In 2008, I was viewed as a somewhat idealistic Confucian thinker who can shed light on politics and everyday life in China. No one doubted my critical perspective and status as an independent scholar. But perceptions started to change in 2012 when I published a comment in the *Financial Times* with Eric Li titled "In Defense of How China Picks Its Leaders." The headline (not chosen by us) was misleading because we argued that China's existing political meritocracy is flawed: "Most obviously, there is widespread corruption in the political system. Term and age limits help to 'guard the guardians,' but more is needed to curb abuses of power, such as a more open and credible media, more transparency and an effective legal system, higher salaries for officials, and more independent anti-corruption agencies."[26] The comment generated a bit of a firestorm and I repeatedly had to emphasize that I'm defending an ideal, not the reality. To help set the record straight, I decided to write a whole book on China's highly imperfect political meritocracy. The book would spell out, in a systematic way, the ideal of political meritocracy and I would expose the gap between the ideal and the reality and propose ways of minimizing the gap. Surely, no one could mistake my critical perspective for a defense of the *status quo* after my book was published! The book, titled *The China Model: Political Meritocracy and the Limits of Democracy*, was published by Princeton University Press in 2015, and it made things even worse. In retrospect, I realize that the problem may lie with the title, selected mainly for marketing reasons, which sounds like a defense of the *status quo*.[27] A more boring title, such as "Political Meritocracy in China: The Ideal Versus the Reality," might have prevented misunderstandings. But it's too late for that. The final nail in the coffin, so to speak, was my job as dean of the School of Political Science and Public Administration at Shandong University. Clearly, if I'm offered such a position, it means that "they" can count on my loyalty and it's impossible for me to develop a critical perspective on contemporary Chinese politics.

I must confess, however, that my own character flaws—hypersensitivity to criticism perceived as unfair and a bit of a paranoid streak, not to mention sheer stupidity—also help to explain why I've been effectively silenced by dominant media outlets in the West. I was locked out of the *Guardian*'s Comment Is Free even before I went "from Confucian to Communist" in people's minds. I wrote a few comments for the *Guardian* but was frustrated by headlines that made me seem like an apologist for the Chinese government. I wrote to the editor to no effect, since, as with other leading media outlets in the West, the editors choose the headlines without consulting authors and the authors have no veto power. Finally, I complained in the comments section of my own comment, adding the line, "Comments may be free but the headlines aren't." The editor deleted my complaint and sent an email with the warning: "We consider this kind of thing defamatory of Cif and its editors." I apologized, meekly, but after that none of my contributions were approved for publication in Comment Is Free.

My collaboration with the *New York Times* ended in an equally dramatic manner. In 2017, however, I was pleasantly surprised that an op-ed editor accepted a comment I wrote about Chinese identity. I argued that "being Chinese" is a matter of culture rather than race. He asked for fact checks before the article was published and I duly sent him the references, ccing Professor P., an academic friend specializing in Chinese history who had helped with the historical parts of the comment. The night before the op-ed was due to be published, however, my editor phoned to say that there was a problem: It seems that I had plagiarized parts of the article. I was shocked! Where's the problem? I asked. He pointed to a couple of factual points, but I explained that I sent him the references in response to his request for fact checking and it's all public information, so why can't we just embed the references I sent in the Internet version? He worried most about a long sentence that drew word for word from Professor P.'s article. I responded, how can it be plagiarized if I mentioned his name before the quotation and had cced him all along? I used a long quotation because I wanted to preserve his original language and thank him for his help! My editor friend asked why I didn't use quotation marks. I was stumped. It occurred to me that I had read thousands of op-eds and written dozens of my own and I had never noticed the convention that sentences or parts of sentences are sometimes embedded in quotation marks. In my academic works, I have tons of footnotes, but the quotation marks are followed with the references. Why hadn't I noticed a different convention for op-eds? I speculated to my editor friend that perhaps it's because quotation marks not followed by references look "naked" to the academic eye. I felt stupid and apologized but I added, Surely you realize that there's no ill intention since I kept Professor P. in the loop on the email chain and he didn't see anything wrong, either. Anyway, we can correct it just by adding a couple of quotation marks around the sentence. I learned my lesson and won't make such stupid mistakes again. My editor said that he'd consult with others at the *New York Times* and get back to me. He phoned a few hours later and told me that they wouldn't publish a plagiarized op-ed. I was not happy: I can accept that they won't publish it because of my honest mistake, but please don't use the word "plagiarism," which signals ill intent to use somebody else's words without acknowledgment and consent. From my point of view, it was a misunderstanding that could easily be corrected by adding a couple of quotation marks. Still, I tried to be polite. I said, Thanks for your help and I'll send it elsewhere for publication. He responded with an email saying that I had committed a serious ethical infraction and I should not publish the piece elsewhere because it would make him feel uneasy. I half-admired his *chutzpah* but was not pleased that he had impugned my integrity. I told him that I have something important to say and I will find a way to publish it. I added some quotation marks around the offending sentence and rewrote the piece without his edits (it took a few minutes) and sent it to the *Wall Street Journal*, which published the comment with the headline "Why Anyone Can Be Chinese."[28] The comment generated lots of interest and controversy and I plan to write my next book on the topic. But it was the end of my publishing experience with the op-ed pages of the *New York Times*.

## A Wish List

I've since lost the drive to be a public intellectual in the West, though I do occasionally publish comments in the Chinese-language media and the (Hong Kong–based) *South China Morning Post* as well as longer essays in new and open-minded U.S.-based periodicals such as *American Affairs* and *American Purpose*.[29] But enough self-pity. Overall, I'm tremendously grateful for the many critical and constructive reviews by academics and journalists in the Western world who engage with my ideas and help push forward the arguments (I'm especially grateful to Princeton University Press for publishing my books uncensored for any political content, in sharp contrast to what's possible in China). Let's go back to the big picture: Public opinion makes it almost impossible to publish comments that offer a balanced picture of Chinese politics in leading Western media outlets. How might things change? People in the West need to allow for the possibility that a political system that does not select top leaders by means of free and fair elections can be morally legitimate and that an economic system can legitimately place substantial constraints on the private accumulation of wealth for the sake of the common good. On China's part, the political system needs to become less repressive and more humane. China should welcome journalists from the West and they should be given free rein to report as they see fit when they're in China. In the case of the *New York Times*, the one reporter on the ground at the height of the Covid pandemic, Keith Bradsher, filed balanced reports informed by local knowledge that provided Anglophone readers with a detailed and nuanced picture of the country.[30] More such stories might help to change public opinion in the West. Informal online reports are equally helpful. The Barretts, a British son and father team, are a good example. As they travel and visit different parts of China, they make insightful and humorous videos and post them online. Hundreds of thousands of international viewers enjoy their representation of the many details that characterize the "real" China. They might err on the excessively positive side, but it's a useful corrective to the negativity in the mainstream media. China is diverse and vibrant, whatever its shortcomings. One of the best ways to show that is to let journalists and people from abroad be the bridges and messengers.[31] More wishful thinking? Perhaps. But it's not crazy to imagine a day when most reports in leading media outlets in the West help to humanize China and when op-ed pages in leading media outlets once again open up to more balanced commentary on Chinese politics.

I'd like to emphasize that I do not mean to equate China's formal system of censorship with the informal system in the

West. It's far worse in China. I dearly hope that China can learn from the norms of academic and media freedom in the West. That said, there may be something to be learned from Chinese-style censorship: The censors are more open when it comes to giving the reason.[32] The editors in China usually tell authors that they can't publish this or that because it's too politically sensitive. In contrast, Western editors will almost never say that they can't publish submissions for political reasons. In my experience, it only happened once: About two decades ago, I submitted an op-ed to the *Asian Wall Street Journal* arguing that sex work should be legalized in China. The editor said that they couldn't publish it because their paper had an editorial policy against legalization of sex work. It was a refreshingly honest response, and I understood. I sometimes wish editors at leading media outlets in the West would just come clean and tell me that they can't publish my submissions because their own editorial policies have become more "anti-CCP" of late. But I guess it's harder to admit to constraining freedom of speech if one is committed to its value.

# 9

# Academic Meritocracy, Chinese-Style

IN AN ELECTORAL DEMOCRACY, it's clear who chooses the political leaders: the people who vote for them. I'm sometimes asked: Who chooses the leaders in a political meritocracy? In China, I respond, only half-jokingly, it's the Organization Department (组织部). The most senior-level appointments are decided by Politburo members. At the lowest level, people usually get to vote for their village leaders. In between, the large bulk of public officials are selected by the Organization Department, which is like the world's largest and most powerful human resources department, responsible for approximately seventy million personnel assignments across all forms and levels of government and state-owned enterprises.[1] The goal, in theory, is to ensure that the most qualified people are selected for political posts, though cynics will add that it also ensures the CCP's hegemony over key aspects of society.

I was surprised to find out that the Organization Department also selects leaders in academia, including my own faculty's leadership. My term as dean started in January 2017 and I learned quickly that the dean didn't have much independent power: All major decisions are made by a group of nine leaders that consisted of five vice-deans, three party secretaries, and myself. There is a clear division of responsibilities among leaders, but we deliberate at length to solve problems, with each leader having some sort of say. Several of us were new on the job and things were a bit awkward at first. After a few years, we became comfortable with one another and developed a more or less stable decision-making system. Nearly five years later, however, I was informed that it was time for a leadership change, and our university's Organization Department would decide on personnel appointments.

How did the Organization Department select our new faculty leaders? They called a meeting with all of our faculty's professors at the rank of associate professor and above. Each member of the collective leadership committee gave a short speech summarizing what we did for the faculty followed by a brief account of research and teaching achievements. Then we were all asked to fill out detailed forms ranking each leader's performance according to criteria such as ability, diligence, and virtue. There were also *pro forma* questions asking about political loyalty to the ruling organization.[2] After a few minutes, the professors lined up to submit their forms in a transparent box (presumably to show that the voting process is clean). The following week, I met with stone-faced members of the Organization Department and I was asked to comment on the other leaders from the outgoing committee. As for myself, I told them that I'd become a symbolic leader; I'd stay on as dean for a year at the most, and we would need to find a replacement. Two weeks later, I was called again to meet with the Organization Department. They presented me with a list of their tentative choices for the new faculty leaders' committee and asked if I had any comments. I said that they seemed like good choices (I was sincere). My interviewers, sitting across the table, asked for some implicit rankings of the vice-deans, presumably to help with the next leadership change. I asked if I could keep the paper with the list of tentative choices and they said, No, it's not official yet. A week later, our faculty was presented with the Organization Department's final decisions of who would serve on the faculty leadership committee for the next five years, including a list of who was responsible for what. It was the same list as the tentative list I had been shown the previous week. Our executive vice-dean had been promoted to a higher-level post in Jinan and a hard-working vice-dean had been selected as his replacement. Our party secretary would continue in his post, and he was now playing a more important role.[3] I was to stay as a dean and my official responsibility was listed as "全面负责学院行政工作," which can be translated as "responsible for the overall administration of the faculty."[4] Our gender ratio improved somewhat: We now had three female leaders, which was triple the number of five years earlier.

What do I make of this selection process? On the one hand, I am impressed by the extent of consultation with different kinds of stakeholders before decisions are finalized. The time-consuming process of gathering viewpoints, by means of formal voting and evaluations as well as informal chats, provided the Organization Department with more than enough material to evaluate the candidates, and they seemed to come up with good choices. I do not know from personal experience how deans and vice-deans are selected in Western universities, but from what I hear the decision-making process is less than democratic, perhaps less so than at Shandong University. On the other hand, the actual decision-making process is somewhat

mysterious. I have no idea how much the voting and evaluations by professors influenced the final decision-making of the
Organization Department. I can speculate that it didn't matter
much in my case, since it had more or less been decided in advance with our university's party secretary the previous year
that I'd stay on for a year or two as symbolic leader. It probably
made some difference in other cases, but I'm not sure how
much. That said, it's worth asking if more transparency is always
desirable. I never did get to see my colleagues' evaluations of
my own record, which came as a bit of a relief because I'd likely
have been demoralized by the result.

I'm reminded of a conversation I had with a leader of the
Organization Department in Shanxi in June 2017.[5] If CCP leaders
are so great, I asked, why not be more open about the leadership
selection process to show that it is as rigorous and meritocratic
as advertised? The Organization Department leader asked how
professors select candidates in academia. I replied that the relevant department establishes a committee that aims to select
the best candidates, and committee members deliberate
among themselves. The leader asked if deliberations are open.
I replied, "Of course not: Open deliberations would set constraints on what's said, nor would it be fair to the candidates
who are not selected." The leader smiled and said, "the same
goes for us." We need to save the face of the candidates who
were not selected. And he explained that the Organization
Department—one of the most prestigious departments in the
Chinese political system—selects its own officials partly according to their ability to keep secrets.[6] So I should not have
been surprised by the secrecy of our faculty's leadership selection process, though I still think the Organization Department could at least be more transparent about which factors
count for how much.

## Exams, Elections, and Evaluations

The selection of students and professors is more directly driven by what we can call "academic meritocracy," meaning that candidates are selected according to actual and potential academic ability. Political loyalty and virtue are not officially part of the decision-making process. As at other Chinese universities, our undergraduate students are selected based on the national university entrance examinations (*gaokao*). The grade on the *gaokao* determines college admission, with very few exceptions.[7] Those who score well often have a choice of faculties, and some of our work as administrators involves persuading students (and, more importantly, their parents) to entice the high performers to come to our faculty. The big obstacle is our name—School of Political Science and Public Administration (政治学与公共管理学院)—because the word "politics" (政治) sounds very boring to high school students who have spent years memorizing political propaganda. We have to persuade prospective students (and their parents) that students learn to think creatively about different social problems and political possibilities and that graduates often find challenging and relatively high-paying jobs in both the public and private sectors. We have spent years deliberating about the possibility of changing our name to the more neutral-sounding School of Government (政府管理学院), like Chinese universities such as Peking University, but we have yet to make the switch for complicated bureaucratic reasons that I do not fully understand.

Graduate students are also selected based on examinations.[8] There is more room for subjective evaluation, however, especially at the oral examination stage, which follows the written examinations. Our professors set the questions and grade the exams, which puts Shandong University undergraduates who are familiar with the system at an advantage. It is almost impossible for a student who didn't score well to get admitted, but once they pass a certain bar senior professors with strong views can often select the students they prefer (as may be the case in leading Western universities).[9] In the West, the most challenging part of being a doctoral student is to produce a high-quality thesis. At our university, it's publishing two academic articles in officially recognized CSSCI (Chinese Social Science Citation Index) journals. This requirement comes from the sciences, where it's common for graduate students to publish works in academic journals, often co-authored with their professors. But it makes little sense in our discipline. Tsinghua's Department of Philosophy abolished this requirement a few years ago. Here, too, our university is unusually resistant to change. I proposed abolishing the requirement but was told it came from the university and our faculty did not have unilateral control over it. In my second year, the requirement was relaxed—it's now okay to co-publish articles with professors—but this change led to another form of abuse: Professors add their names to papers written almost entirely by their students simply in order to help them graduate (I confess I occasionally participated in this practice because otherwise the papers by my graduate students wouldn't get published). At some point, we do need to move to a system where graduate students are evaluated first and foremost on the quality of their theses.

As for professors, they are selected and promoted by an academic committee in our faculty (they must also be approved at a higher stage by a university-wide committee that rarely rejects our choices). The committee consists of fourteen professors elected by associate professors and above in our faculty (we have about seventy such professors). It's a hugely important committee and most of us feel honored to be elected to the committee by our peers. We had one meeting to select new members two years into my term as dean (before that, I could attend the meetings but without voting rights). Everyone was entitled to one vote and I was impressed by the transparent process—all the votes were tabulated one at a time in front of the whole faculty, presumably to allay fears of vote-tampering—but I also felt bad for professors who came out at the bottom, which seemed like a big loss of face and may have exacerbated their sense of alienation from the faculty (ideally, only the winners would be announced and the vote counters would be trusted to keep things honest). To my great relief, the dean was exempted from the voting process because I was automatically appointed to the academic committee without having to be voted in by fellow professors. It seemed to be an *ad hoc* decision at the time, but I think the other leaders thought it was more important to save my face than to show commitment to full democracy in the faculty.

Academic meritocracy is most evident in the hiring process. Like the practice in Western universities, candidates are evaluated first and foremost according to academic ability. We look at résumés and letters of recommendation and the candidates are interviewed by the academic committee (in person before Covid, online after Covid for candidates who couldn't come to our campus). That said, political considerations do intervene at times. Candidates who are party members display this fact on their résumés (we don't discuss this criterion in our deliberations, but there is an assumption that such candidates are smart and tend to be good at cooperating with other people). In principle, potential hires could be vetoed on political grounds. Such cases are rare in my faculty, but they do happen. Shortly after Donald Trump's election as president of the United States (before I was dean), we were considering hiring a well-known

Chinese professor teaching in a Western country, but he was vetoed at some stage. I asked a confidant if it was because he was anti-CCP. I was told, No, the problem is that he's too anti-American. I laughed and said, Many Americans are anti-American since Trump's election. My confidant replied, We worry about extremists, regardless of ideology. In another case, a foreign candidate had a good interview and we went out for dinner afterward with several members of the academic committee and a party secretary. The candidate couldn't hold his liquor well and he argued for more American intervention in the East Asian region on the grounds that Chinese influence is so pernicious. The more he drank, the less respect he showed to my Chinese colleagues. He heaped praise on me, saying I was the only one, as a foreigner, who could express my true views. After the dinner, the party secretary and a couple of my colleagues privately expressed strong dissatisfaction. We didn't pursue his case.

The academic committee also decides on the promotion of colleagues. Here, we need to make sure that colleagues are promoted based on academic ability rather than personal friendships or connections (关系) with other members of the faculty. We are quite rigid when it comes to assessing academic ability: We look at research output, as measured by SSCI (Social Science Citation Index) English-language academic publications in the West and CSSCI (Chinese Social Science Citation Index) Chinese-language academic publications in China.[10] The former are given more weight because there is an assumption (correct, in most cases) that publishing in Chinese-language academic publications is more influenced by personal connections with the editors. But this means that professors who publish high-quality works in Chinese but cannot write well in English are penalized relative to professors who write well in English (somewhat ironic, given that the country as a whole is supposed to be moving in a more nationalist direction with more pride in Chinese language and culture).

The system for promotion is far from ideal if the aim is to assess academic merit. For one thing, committee members don't read most of the candidates' publications. Candidates are assessed according to quantitative output, meaning the number of publications in academic journals that are ranked according to some external assessment of quality. Second, books are not given much weight. The bias against books comes from the Chinese experience: Academic publishers are not particularly well regarded (in the past, it was common for academics to pay publishers to publish their works) and publishers do not have a rigorous external review process to ensure quality control. I try to persuade some of my colleagues to publish in prestigious university presses in the West, but the effort may not be rewarded for younger colleagues so I can't push too hard. Third, it's necessary, in most cases, for candidates considered for promotion to have obtained government-funded research grants (项目). Such grants place more emphasis on contribution to the country's needs (as determined by political leaders) than on academic contribution. Sometimes, intellectually mediocre applications are awarded grants mainly because they conform to the political ideology of the day (such as Xi Jinping's thought). In addition, short articles published in politically prestigious newspapers such as the *People's Daily* and the *Guangming Daily* are counted as the equivalent of academic publications (to be fair, it's extremely difficult to publish in these newspapers, but they do not select articles according to academic merit). Last but not least, increased censorship means that it's difficult for some talented professors to publish their research. More and more research areas in political science are considered off-limits. I get many complaints, especially from young professors, that they can no longer publish research on topics such as social protests in China even if the findings are relatively favorable to the government. Fortunately, academics are free to publish politically sensitive material in English-language publications, but here, too, talented Chinese professors who do not write well in English are at a disadvantage. I try to help by suggesting translators, but it's costly for young professors (if I were to provide translation services myself, it would be a full-time job).[11]

## Chinese Academia as Number One?

Notwithstanding such problems, I'm still optimistic regarding our faculty's academic future, and perhaps Chinese academia more generally. Our new hires are generally outstanding. They are often trained abroad and can write high-quality academic works in both Chinese and English.[12] Why do we get better and better professors at the same time that increased political constraints negatively affect academic work in China? At our university, it's partly explained by higher salaries and the attraction of a beautiful seaside campus with nearby subsidized apartments for all professors. Push factors matter, too. It's getting harder to find good academic jobs abroad, and academics from China experience increasing discrimination in Western countries. The anti-China turn in the West has benefited our faculty because it is easier to recruit talented young Chinese professors who completed their doctoral studies abroad. In the past, overseas PhDs might have hoped to get jobs abroad, but they are increasingly discouraged by the anti-China sentiment in Western countries (if Chinese academics do seek jobs abroad, they need to conceal their positive evaluations of the Chinese government). Another reason for optimism is that faculties and universities within China constantly compete for upgrades in national and international rankings. The Ministry of Education literally grades faculties according to academic performance (here too, the number of academic publications is the key factor). Our faculty was given a B+ in 2017 and we developed a detailed plan to raise it to A+ by the year 2025. If we succeed, it means downgrades for similar faculties in other Chinese universities since there are a limited number of top "grades."[13] The effect of this intense competition is to put constant pressure on academics to publish more and on administrators to attract more talented professors.[14]

Overall, I am confident that we will continue to improve academically, and I can only hope that political constraints will diminish over time. That said, I do want to question the premise that academic ability and output are the only things that matter for universities. Chinese universities, almost all of which are public institutions, strongly emphasize the obligation to serve the country and the world as a whole.[15] Shandong University's official slogan is "为天下储人才, 为国家图富强," which can be roughly translated as "accumulating talent for the world and making the country strong and prosperous." So if our academic output did not have a positive social influence, we would have failed in our mission. The challenge is how to encourage high-quality academic research that helps society without the propaganda and censorship that make academics miserable.

# 10

# A Critique of Cuteness

IN A BID TO SHAPE international public opinion about China, President Xi Jinping told senior officials that the country needed to present a more "credible, loveable, and respectable" image of China.[1] This surprising formulation is more than a call to tame down the "Wolf Warrior" rhetoric. The key word is "可爱" (*ke ai*).[2] *Ke ai* literally means "can love" and it is translated by official media as "lovable." But *ke ai* means "cute" in everyday usage.

The idea of "cuteness" as soft power may seem odd on the face of it. But the rapid spread of what we can term the "culture of cuteness"—a public affirmation of cute animals, robots, and emojis that inform everyday social interaction—is one of the most fascinating social developments in contemporary China. The trend started in Japan in the 1970s—when the country was largely ruled by bureaucrats meritocratically selected from an ultra-competitive educational system. The culture of cuteness was led by teenage girls and eventually filtered to other sectors of society. Over the past decade or so, it has spread to China almost like wildfire. The streets of Chinese cities are populated with ridiculously cute dogs and cats, and the use of cute emojis has become the norm for communication on social media, even in official settings such as exchanges between bureaucrats. In Shanghai's not-so-cold winters, it has become almost compulsory to clothe cute small dogs with colorful jackets, to the point that it becomes somewhat jarring to spot a "naked" dog walking the streets.[3]

It's worth asking why the culture of cuteness has planted social roots so quickly and deeply in China.[4] One explanation is cultural. The use of cute emojis in digital conversation may be more widespread in East Asian countries that prioritize politeness and indirect talk because online communication cannot be softened by facial expressions of deference or hierarchical rituals such as bowing. Hence, East Asians like to use cute or funny images to relax the communication atmosphere and minimize the risk of misunderstandings or hurting other people's feelings.[5]

The meritocratic social and political systems also help to explain the culture of cuteness. According to one study, viewing cute images promotes careful behavior and narrows attentional focus, with potential benefits for learning and office work.[6] Cute images make it easier to concentrate, and so may help those vying for success in ultra-competitive societies. But the culture of cuteness also represents a kind of rebellion against the whole system: Instead of affirming the value of boring and hard-working (largely male) meritocratically selected bureaucrats who serve the public good, it affirms the value of playful and somewhat self-indulgent ways of life. As Simon May puts it in his brilliant and highly entertaining book *The Power of Cute*, the culture of cuteness articulates "a nascent will to repudiate the ordering of human relations by power, or at least to question our assumptions about who has power and to what end. This is a will that Cute can vividly convey precisely because it usually involves a relationship to a vulnerable object or to an object that flaunts, or flirts with, vulnerability. It is a will to liberation from the power paradigm that many, especially in the West and Japan, but perhaps ordinary Chinese people too, might be expected to affirm as an antidote to a century and more of unparalleled brutality."[7]

If the culture of cuteness is (at least partly) a reaction against an ultra-competitive meritocratic political system underpinned by an ultra-competitive educational system, one might expect the culture of cuteness not to have substantial impact in more easygoing, less competitive societies. This hypothesis is supported by the fact that the culture of cuteness has had little social impact in the world's happiest countries, such as Denmark and Finland. In China, it's not uncommon for tough-looking guys to carry the cute red or gold purses of their girlfriends. I once spotted a full-grown man in Shanghai holding a balloon in one hand and licking an ice cream in the other. A male professor at Shandong University walks around with a T-shirt that has bling-bling pictures of cute pink teddy bears. Such scenes are unheard of in supposedly more open Western societies. In Western societies, such symbols are interpreted as signaling sexual interest in same-sex partners rather than paying winking homage to the culture of cuteness.

Given that the culture of cuteness seems so closely tied to the Chinese (or East Asian) context, why would President Xi affirm the need to promote the image of a "cute" China abroad?[8] It might seem like a losing cause outside of East Asia, especially in Western societies that pride themselves on commitment to Enlightenment values of rationality and scientific (i.e., not cute) approaches to life. But the culture of cuteness also has universal reach. The cute cat unifies warring tribes on the global Internet. More surprisingly, perhaps, a herd of fifteen wild elephants in China's Yunnan Province has joined the big family of cuteness.

Western media outlets that normally report on doom and gloom in China actively documented the unusual trek of this seemingly lost and aimless herd of elephants.[9]

There is a political dimension to this story—the protected habitats for elephants may no longer support the growing numbers of elephants[10]—but the main reason for the media attention is that people are naturally attracted to cuteness. Humans tend to be moved by beautiful animals that express a seeming vulnerability. Cat lovers know that it's impossible to be bored by a beautiful cat face. The elephant story, however, is a reminder that cuteness is not the same as beauty. Elephants, with their intimidating size and parched skin, are far from the most beautiful animals. But they can still exhibit the quality of cuteness when they are lost and appear to be vulnerable and in need of help. Cute animals, even if ugly, arouse the same sentiments of care we have for vulnerable (and often awkward and silly-looking) human babies. The star of the elephant herd in Yunnan was a baby elephant born during the herd's trek to nowhere. In a drone video seen around the world, the baby sleeping in the middle of the herd wakes up and adorably struggles to climb out from among the larger elephants.[11] Another time, the baby elephant fell into a ditch and his mother helped to dig him out. Here too, it was impossible not to sympathize with his predicament.[12] Mencius famously said that we feel natural empathy for the suffering of a child about to fall into a well, but we feel the same empathy for a cute animal that needs to be rescued.[13]

So that's the good part. When cuteness is confined to the animal world, there's nothing wrong. Who can object to an adorable and vulnerable-looking baby elephant? But when cuteness is used for social and political purposes in the human world, it's easy for things for go wrong. Consider what could have happened to the wandering elephants. As it turns out, it was a success story for China's soft power. Local inhabitants worked closely with public officials to secure the elephants' well-being and the herd eventually returned "home." It shows that, when things go well, it's often impossible to separate the people from the CCP, whatever the propaganda from abroad. But what if the story had ended badly? What if the baby elephant had died or if an elephant had killed humans? Local officials would have been worried about being blamed and they might have followed the example of Wuhan officials when Covid broke out: Try to cover up the mess. But word would eventually have leaked out and the foreign press would have gleefully reported what went wrong. So China's soft-power victory would have turned into a defeat. Cuteness as soft power can be effective only if it's accompanied by credible news reporting, but how can news be credible if the government tries to cover up bad news?

Cuteness as a human virtue, in other words, is not sufficient: It needs to be accompanied by other virtues to be positive in its social effects. At the very least, it needs to be constrained by an aversion to cruelty. Some cat owners in China make their pets undergo a painful operation to cut single eyelids into larger (and supposedly cuter) double eyelids.[14] Double eyelid surgery is the most common form of plastic surgery for women in East Asian countries (to the point that it's rare to see single eyelids in wealthy neighborhoods), and who am I to object to local conceptions of beauty? But it crosses a moral line when pets are forced to undergo such an operation.

For ordinary citizens, the culture of cuteness has an important function, especially in East Asian societies with a Confucian heritage. Perhaps the deepest problem with Confucianism is the assumption that the best form of life involves serving the political community *qua* public official. It helps to explain why public officials in China, from members of the Politburo to minor bureaucrats in the remote countryside, have such high social status. The downside, however, is that those without political power may not feel a sense of (equal) social worth. So, there is a need to devalue the social contribution of the professional public official. It may be important, but it's not the only way (or necessarily the best way) to lead a meaningful social life nor is it to the only way (or necessarily the best way) to make a social contribution. This shouldn't be too controversial: It should be obvious, for example, that my social contribution *qua* bureaucrat is minor compared to, say, the heroic doctors and nurses in Wuhan. There is a need to affirm the social value of "nonpolitical" ways of life that contribute to the social good, such as the work of health workers and family caretakers. The culture of cuteness also has an important role to play in legitimizing alternative avenues for socially valuable ways of life. Even if cuteness doesn't involve promoting people's well-being in a direct and self-conscious way, it gives meaning to the lives of those left out of political hierarchies and brings a sense of joy and fun to people's lives.

But here, too, cuteness can be dangerous on its own. If it goes too far in devaluing political participation by ordinary people and affirming "non-political" forms of life, it may leave ordinary citizens more exposed to manipulation or oppression by the state. John Stuart Mill famously worried "that so few now dare to be eccentric marks the chief danger of our time"[15]—he thought eccentrics expressed alternatives to the *status quo*, and hence paved the way for social progress—but eccentricity can also take the form of depoliticized cuteness. Shanghai, for example, is ground zero for the culture of cuteness in China, but its "city-zens" are far less willing to talk politics or to criticize the government than the not-so-cute "city-zens" of Beijing.[16]

Commitment to the culture of cuteness, in other words, also needs to be accompanied by a commitment to some form of democratic participation by ordinary citizens. Too much cuteness can also undermine the ideal of political meritocracy, meaning a political system that aims to select and promote public officials with the ability and motivation to serve the political community. If citizens really come to believe that serving the public in a direct way does not matter much, and people of talent and virtue no longer seek to go into government, China's ruling organization will become a mediocrity, not to mention that my own university will lose the talented and hard-working administrators I admire so much. So yes, the life of the bureaucrat may not be the best life, but it should still be recognized as an important form of life. It's fine for the culture of cuteness to affirm alternative forms of life, but it needs to be complemented by more political conceptions of the good life.

Surprisingly, perhaps, the culture of cuteness has also infiltrated the bureaucracy in China. One might think of the boring bureaucrat as the antithesis of cuteness. But here at Shandong University, we all strive to be cute. In my WeChat exchanges with fellow administrators, we try to outdo one another with cute emojis that express our emotions, a trend that has only accelerated since working at home during the virus scare (I once asked a professor friend at Harvard about practices there, and he said that it's inconceivable that professors would exchange cute messages with university administrators). Cute emojis help to avoid misunderstandings and liven up otherwise boring exchanges (my favorite emojis are those of Marx and Confucius with different facial expressions). But there's a serious risk for newcomers such as myself. In response to a cup of coffee emoji, I sent the shit emoji by mistake to a colleague, thinking it was chocolate ice-cream. It's hard to make up for such mistakes, which would never occur in everyday speech. Another mistake took more than two years to correct. I often ended my WeChat messages with an emoji of a smiley face. Finally, my ever-polite assistant grew exasperated. He explained that the smiley face does not represent cheerfulness or happy agreement. Quite the opposite: It conveys sarcasm or even hostility because the eyes are not affected the way they would be with a genuine smile.[17] Now I use the correct emoji of a smiley face with smiling eyes.

Even more worrisome, the culture of cuteness can be used to avoid responsibility. It's not a great sin for teenage girls, but it can be a disaster for public officials who often need to make hard decisions and take responsibility for those decisions.[18] Cuteness can be used as an excuse for taking the easy route, even if it leads to disaster. The cutest political leader in modern times (in my humble estimation) is the United Kingdom's former prime minister Boris Johnson. It's hard not to be charmed by his tousled hair, confused look, and self-deprecating sense of humor. He appears to be somewhat vulnerable, as though he's in need of the help of fellow citizens to get things done. It may be an act, but it often works. We can argue about whether Brexit was a good idea, but the vote took place without much informed deliberation and Johnson helped pushed it through with his cuteness. Worse, Johnson as prime minister acted far too late to deal with Covid. He was guided by his libertarian instincts, which flew in the face of scientific advice—and his reluctance to make the hard decision to lock down the country, reluctance that befits a "cute" prime minister, contributed to the (otherwise avoidable) deaths of thousands of people.[19] Conversely, no one doubts the "ethic of responsibility" of not-so-cute political leaders such as Germany's former chancellor Angela Merkel or China's president Xi Jinping. Their decisions may not always be ideal, but they won't refuse to take responsibility by playing cute.[20]

Let me end this essay with another round of self-criticism. Shortly before I assumed the deanship at Shandong University, I received a shocking email from a former doctoral student at Tsinghua. He was helping a visiting professor I had invited to find accommodation on campus, but things went wrong and the visitor was given poorer than expected living quarters. I expressed disappointment with the outcome in an email. It's worth quoting the former student's emailed response at length:

> You are the inviter of Prof [X], not me, not [Y], not [Z], not any of your students or friends. So you're supposed to be the one who knows better about everything than others. You're supposed to be the one who takes the real responsibilities. You're supposed to be the one who's most capable of fixing things. Well, what's more: you're supposed to be the last one who has the right to be "disappointed" . . .
>
> I guess, in the world, if there's someone who can speak such harsh words above to you, that would be me. Life is tough? Changes are difficult? Think about me. Don't get me wrong: what I'm trying to say here is rather simple: if I can take care of a visiting professor at Tsinghua, you're supposed to be able to do that all on your own too. Not to mention that, again, you are the inviter. You are the host. Do not be too used to acting like a guest.
>
> And another quick tip: most of the time, being cute cannot make anything better. Always fix the problems in the most direct way. Keep growing up. Do not be a giant baby—I complained to my boss yesterday that the most overwhelming part of teamwork is baby-sitting. Frankly speaking, at that moment, I also thought about you.

When I received this email, I was flabbergasted because the student had been relatively polite in the past. The email seemed so over the top: I had asked the student to help and thanked him but added that I was a bit disappointed with the outcome. What's wrong with delegating some authority? Shortly thereafter, he sent an email asking for forgiveness: "Please allow me to sincerely apologize to you! All those harmful words were just spoken from a drunk mind, rather than a considerate heart." I accepted the apology and moved on. But I wish I had done some introspection at the time. I now realize that I carried the habit of cuteness into my deanship as a way of shirking responsibility. To be fair (to myself), I didn't have to make too many hard decisions because my faculty has lots of resources. Unlike universities elsewhere that face cutbacks, our main task is to figure out how to spend our money. We try to recruit talented professors and students and make many offers, not all of which are accepted. And we don't have a policy of firing professors and administrators who don't perform well. In principle, there is a kind of tenure system, but we have yet to deny anyone tenure. Still, faculty leaders sometimes have to decide between conflicting interests and points of view at our bi-weekly meetings— say, who should get this or that prize or fellowship—and I rarely participated in such debates. When I did, I often resorted to a witty remark that served to deflect the discussion. Not surprisingly, my colleagues would rarely come to me for help.[21] Surely, the main task of a good dean is to help others: students, teachers, and administrators in the faculty and the university as a whole. In that sense, I failed to be a responsible dean because I "played cute."

By the time this book is published, I will (in all likelihood) no longer be dean. I will be an academic who teaches, reads, and writes books. Here too—I can safely predict—I won't be immune from the downside of the culture of cuteness. Cute people are adorable but they exhibit one sin: vanity. Consider the clothed dogs in Shanghai. Their owners spend a lot of time finding colorful outfits and they proudly display the cute dogs to the public (I can't confirm this, but I have a feeling that some cute dogs are as vain as their owners). I'm reminded of a conversation with a Buddhist friend. He asked me what I get from academia. What's the point, ultimately, of being an academic? I confessed that it's not about the sorts of things I'm supposed to care about *qua* bureaucrat: "academic GDP," meaning how well our faculty is rated relative to others in China, the number of citations in SSCI and CSSCI journals,[22] prestigious research grants, and so on. For me, it's not about that. I take pride in teaching students and helping them to flourish. The Confucian test of academic success, I half-joked, is how many students show up at my funeral. I added, more seriously, that I hope to be remembered for my books. My Buddhist friend shook his head and said, "So vain, so vain." I guess I'll just have to take that hit. If I can quote the great (now deceased) American sociologist Daniel Bell, "vanity is the least bad human sin."[23]

# The Case for Symbolic Leadership

CHINA ABOLISHED THE imperial system in 1912. But the ideal of monarchy didn't die. The Confucian reformist Kang Youwei argued for the establishment of a symbolic monarch bound by constitutional constraints. The cause was set back when Kang participated in the abortive restoration of the Qing ruler in 1917, and the Chinese Communist Party's victory in 1949 seemed to deliver the fatal blow to the system of monarchical rule. But the revival of Confucianism has led to the reconsideration of ideals and institutions from China's imperial past. The contemporary Confucian thinker Jiang Qing, inspired by Kang Youwei, strongly defends the ideal of symbolic monarchy as appropriate for contemporary China. Jiang recognizes that it is difficult to re-establish a monarchical system in countries (such as China) that abolished their monarchies, but he argues that a symbolic monarch in today's China can be legitimate in the eyes of the people if the monarch has a noble and ancient lineage, if the lineage is political in nature, if it can be shown that the lineage is direct and unbroken, if the lineage is so unique as to exclude competition from other lineages, and if the citizens universally respect and accept the person with noble political lineage. Jiang shows that descendants of past Emperors cannot meet those conditions (here he differs from Kang Youwei). He then goes through each condition and argues that only one person qualifies as the symbolic monarch in today's China: "the direct heir of Confucius."[1]

## The Beauty of Symbolic Monarchy

Such proposals, admittedly, seem odd. Jiang can't publish his works in mainland China because they are viewed as too politically sensitive.[2] Among Chinese intellectuals otherwise sympathetic to dissident views, Jiang is widely regarded as an anachronistic reactionary. In principle, however, it might be argued that symbolic rule is a good idea, especially where it currently exists. Consider the British monarchy, where the reigning monarch exercises symbolic power and the political leader makes actual policy. The most obvious case for symbolic monarchy is that most people endorse the institution. In the United Kingdom in 2021, 62 percent of citizens supported the monarchy.[3] But there are worrisome signs for the future. The same poll shows that younger age groups are much more likely to oppose the monarchy. In Canada, only one-third of citizens preferred Canada to remain a monarchy and 43 percent said recent events show that the royal family holds racist views.[4] Still, it doesn't mean we should ditch the monarchy. Burkean conservatives remind us "that good things are easier to destroy than to preserve, and hard to recover once they have been lost."[5] If it's true that the monarchy has been colored by racism, the proper response is to reform the institution rather than abolish it. President George Washington was a slaveholder, but the appropriate response would have been to abolish slavery rather than the elected presidency.

Nor is it just a matter of holding on to historical legacies. There are powerful arguments in favor of symbolic monarchy that help to explain why constitutional monarchies are relatively successful in the contemporary world: Nine of the eleven most enduring constitutions are constitutional monarchies and many of the world's richest countries are constitutional monarchies.[6] As Tom Ginsburg, Dan Rodriguez, and Barry Weingast argue, monarchs symbolically integrate diverse populations and tend to assume a special role as defenders of all their subjects, including minorities: Constitutional monarchs made a special point of protecting Jewish subjects during World War II.[7] Monarchs can reassure conservatives that old ways of life are protected, thus keeping them on board even in times of fast modernization: General MacArthur's decision to preserve the Emperor induced conservatives in postwar Japan to cooperate with the Occupation authorities and allowed the successful reconstruction of Japan, including radical land reform that would otherwise have been opposed. Constitutional monarchies can also reduce the likelihood of populist politics: "With the presence of a monarch, there is no way a populist can claim to be the one true leader representing the entire people."[8] Hence, it's no coincidence that populists such as Recep Tayyip Erdoğan or Hugo Chavez emerge in countries without symbolic monarchs.

The psychological secret to symbolic monarchy is the separation of powers. We tend to think of the separation of powers as the separation of legislative, executive, and judicial powers. But it's equally, if not more, important to separate the two most important powers of the head of state: the power to make political decisions for the good of the whole country and the symbolic, ritualistic power to represent the state in official ceremonies. In the United States and China, the two powers are merged in one person: the president. In the United Kingdom and Canada, they are separated. The monarch has symbolic, ritualistic power, and the elected prime minister has the power to decide on policy (with the support of his or her party and the majority of the House of Commons).

Other things being equal, the separation of symbolic and political powers is a good idea. The symbolic monarch can spend his or her time on rituals. Success does not depend too much on talent. In the United Kingdom, the monarch's task is mainly to appear contented, read speeches written by others, and greet visiting heads of state. He may not be the most brilliant person in the room, but it doesn't matter. Nor could he abuse his power even if he wanted to. He is not supposed to interfere in policy making. And since the symbolic monarch represents the state, including past and future generations, he can exert a pull on people's emotions. Citizens can project their love of country onto him, while being more rational in evaluating the decisions of the elected prime minister. Meanwhile, the top political decision-maker can spend her time thinking about appropriate policies benefiting the country. She need not waste time cutting ribbons and officiating at national ceremonies.

Conversely, it's much easier for things to go wrong in political systems that merge symbolic and political powers at the highest level of government. In the United States and China, the president of the country is both the channel for people's emotions and the most important political decision-maker. So citizens are more likely to support bad decisions by the political leader since he or she also represents the state as a whole.[9] There is no other channel for people's emotions at the top and citizens are less likely to critically evaluate the decisions of the leader. Even worse, the leader in a merged political system can create a cult of personality that's dangerous for the long-term good of the state. It's not a new argument. As James Hankins explains, the Renaissance humanist thinker Francesco Patrizi "explicitly criticizes Alexander the Great for attempting to create a ruler-cult around himself; following this false counsel of prudence, he remarks, was one reason Alexander's dynasty did not outlast him. He instead praises the Persians in the time of King Cyrus (as described in Xenophon's *Cyropaedia*) for resisting the temptation to divinize their ruler."[10] In the United States, a large chunk of citizens project their patriotic love of country onto the former (and possibly future) president Donald Trump, regardless of how incompetent or morally debased he may be. In China, President Xi abolished presidential term limits and cultivates a cult of personality that celebrates his own thought. It's hard to be optimistic about the long-term prospects of any country with a personality cult at the top, even if we like the policies of rulers in merged systems. If citizens project their emotions onto the political ruler, will the political system appear to be less legitimate once the ruler "joins Karl Marx," as they used to say in China?

## Symbolic Leadership at Lower Levels of "Government"

My first term as dean was due to end in 2020. In the last year, my job consisted almost entirely of symbolic rituals. Internationalization was dead in the water due to Covid and I had hardly any work of substance. I hosted dinners for visitors and participated in welcoming and graduation ceremonies. I learned to talk like a typical Chinese bureaucrat—flat affect and stick to three points, regardless of the substance of what's communicated[11]—but it was mainly "propaganda" (宣传 *xuanchuan*) for our faculty, such as short speeches to parents of first-year students before the start of the academic year to assure them that we'd take good care of their (adult) children. I slowly disengaged from other work and found excuses not to join the marathon faculty leaders' meetings. My identity *qua* symbolic leader was now clear: As my wife put it, I became the faculty panda.

I do not mean to question the value of symbolic rituals for leaders. Quite the opposite. The case for symbolic rituals may be clearer at the highest level of government.[12] The remarkable longevity and constitutional stability of the Republic of Venice, as Edward Muir has explained, was achieved "through a pious, intensely conservative adherence to ritual and legend, a habit that rendered the political order both mystical and sanctified."[13] Consider what happens when leaders stop performing rituals. There's one famous example in the history of China: Emperor Wanli, who reigned from 1572 to 1620. As documented in Ray Huang's excellent book *1587, a Year of No Significance: The Ming Dynasty in Decline*, the most important tasks for the Chinese sovereign were personnel management and ceremonial procedure. The highly intelligent and sensitive Wanli, however, slowly became disenchanted when he could not get his way on key decisions, such as selecting a successor. In the last two decades of his rule, he basically went on strike, withdrawing from public life and refusing to play the Emperor's role in government, leading to widespread alienation that contributed to the end of the Ming Dynasty. In retrospect, the problem was not so much that he withdrew from the "substantial" task of personnel management, since much of that work could be done by meritocratically selected public officials in the bureaucracy. The main problem was his failure to oversee the "symbolic" work of ritualistic proceedings that could not be overseen by anyone else. It's perhaps understandable why the Emperor, who "lost much of his personal identity and had little private life," might want to rebel.[14] Rituals were extremely taxing, if not completely exhausting. But such rituals were invested with (belief in) a cosmic spirit that kept the empire going, as noted by the First Grand Secretary at the time:

> In providing the best leadership to an empire such as ours, there was no substitute for ritualistic proceedings. The emperor did not have a formidable army at his command; he did not even have a very large land base. He remained the Son of Heaven only because everyone believed he was. This belief required the ritualistic exercises involving the sovereign and his chief ministers to be enacted with vigor and regularity, completely in a public spirit, and accompanied by aesthetic and moral overtones. Pageantry or not, the many rounds of kowtowing reaffirmed imperial supremacy; yet merely the fact the emperor attended the ceremonies indicated that he was subjecting himself to the cosmic order and moral law. It was precisely because the messages taken from the basic classical sources were dull and trite that one must be prepared to listen to them again and again. The heat and cold and the pre-dawn hour only tested the human will. This idea of discipline and endurance had been emphasized by Censor Keng. Even in the emperor's farming ritual obviously a degree of make-believe was involved; but make-believe is not necessarily unreal. One must realize how powerful an instrument of government it was when all participants shared a belief in it.[15]

So when Emperor Wanli neglected his symbolic duties, he shattered the "magical" edifice that underpinned the whole system. To use contemporary language, the Emperor's participation in ritual proceedings made others believe that the political system was legitimate, and the system could not survive for long without this belief.

Perhaps now we can better appreciate the work of my favorite monarch, Queen Elizabeth II: It's both extremely difficult and extremely important to serve as a symbolic ruler. As Queen Mary put it to Elizabeth before she was formally anointed in the (semi-fictitious) show *The Crown*, "To do nothing is the hardest job of all. And it will take every ounce of energy that you have; to be impartial is not natural, not human." I'm aware that the stakes are not so high for a minor bureaucrat with symbolic responsibilities, but I did seek direct inspiration from the Queen when participating in ritualistic ceremonies. Doing nothing is hard work! Consider distributing certificates to graduating students. We—the leaders—need to stand straight for three hours without a bathroom break and hand out certificates to hundreds of students. We wear colorful outfits that draw on a mixture of Western and Chinese traditions, with different colors corresponding to different hierarchies in the administration (deans wear red and black, and I confess that I envy the university president and university party secretary, who wear yellow robes, similar to the Emperor's standard costume). We can't show our preferences. I try not to show my enthusiasm when I meet my own students and try not to respond to smiling faces. I have to say "congratulations" (祝贺 *zhuhe*) to each student and sound equally enthusiastic every time.

My personal history adds unexpected challenges. The Chinese national anthem is played at the start of every major ceremony. I first heard the anthem in May and June 1989, when it was played by students in Oxford campaigning for democracy in China who aimed to show how much they cared for the future of the country. This was also the time I met my first love (we married a year later). The music is beautiful and I cried along with others when Chinese students sang it after the killings on June 4. The same emotions, associated with (failed) revolution and (faded) love, come back whenever I hear the anthem. I try to control my emotions in public, if only because it would look strange if a foreigner cried upon hearing the Chinese anthem. I confess, however, that I lost control at one graduation ceremony several months after my divorce. The anthem triggered earlier memories and I could not stifle the tears. After the ceremony, I told my superiors that the tears were triggered by an allergy to my cat.

My first contract as dean expired at the end of 2020 and I expected to hand off to my successor and return to full-time teaching, reading, and writing. I experimented with outer kingship (外王 *wai wang*) and did my best, but discovered that it was not my calling. It's not because I felt disdain for the system. Quite the opposite. In theory, it's hard to improve upon our system for governing a large faculty. There is a clear division of leadership, with different leaders in charge of different aspects and bi-weekly meetings to share notes about work done and how to solve problems. It's not always efficient (to say the least), but we can avoid transparently bad decisions because none would survive the collective deliberations. And I have great admiration for the leaders who tirelessly work for the good of the faculty. Westerners often make fun of Chinese public officials assiduously taking notes at meetings, but it's a deeply embedded aspect of a bureaucratic culture that values learning, hard work, and problem solving.[16] They—we—spend most of our workdays discussing "small" matters such as office space as well as "big" issues such as fifteen-year plans to improve our faculty. I just didn't have the energy to continue. When I told our party secretary that I would prefer to return to teaching and research, however, he wouldn't let me go. I told him that I had become "only" a symbolic leader and it was time to let others serve as dean. But he said it would look bad if I were to leave at that point. Canada-China relations were in a terrible state and it would look as though I had been purged for political reasons.[17] And he flattered me, saying that I was good for the reputation of our faculty.

I consulted a confidant in the faculty. He said that I was good for the faculty precisely because I became a symbolic leader sitting (and doing nothing) above the fray, which helped maintain harmony in the faculty and reduced the factionalism that had plagued us in the past (leaders of factions rarely came to me to complain, unlike in my first couple of years, when I thought that I could get things done). He invoked the Daoist/Legalist view of leadership that power can be increased precisely by doing nothing most of the time. The idea is that the leader accumulates mystique by doing nothing and when he does intervene (as Deng Xiaoping did with his famous endorsement in 1992 of the Shenzhen-style model of market-driven economic growth), the people listen. Also, by not intervening too frequently, the leader does not show his desires, and hence can't be manipulated by ministers or other underlings. If need be, I could effectively intervene to "save" our faculty in times of crisis, just as the Thai monarch helped to defuse civil strife and restore democracy in 1992. Here too, I was flattered but recognized that I really had become a purely symbolic leader who did not intervene and did not plan to intervene even on rare occasions. There was no master or hidden plan to accumulate power and use it when necessary.

Inspired by the Queen—*my* Queen (I'm a Canadian citizen)—I accepted K. *shuji*'s offer to continue to serve as dean. I told him that I'd do the symbolic work only for a year or two, and meanwhile we should prepare a successor. It's worth asking why Queen Elizabeth clung on to (symbolic) power until the very end. In her last few years, she did not, arguably, have sufficient energy to do nothing. King Charles III may be flawed, but (to my mind) he's good on balance and has the energy necessary to perform the "hardest job" of acting as impartial, symbolic ruler. After my failed attempt to resign as symbolic leader, however, it occurred to me that the Queen may also have faced behind-the-scenes obstacles that prevented the handover to her son. If so, my admiration would only be reinforced. How can one not revere a symbolic leader who is "forced" to do exhausting work leading ritual ceremonies well into her nineties?

What about the prospects of reviving symbolic monarchy in China? It doesn't look good for the foreseeable future: Government officials scoff at the idea, as do most intellectuals. I've yet to meet a young person in China who champions monarchy. But things can change in the future (few predicted the reestablishment of the Spanish constitutional monarchy in 1978). I did once meet a descendant of a former Manchu princess in Hong Kong who harbored the hope that her family might be brought back to (symbolic) power. But she seemed eccentric, to say the least. Jiang Qing's proposal that the direct descendant of Confucius should assume the throne may be slightly more plausible, but it's also problematic: There is a risk that the direct descendant of Confucius will lack talent and virtue or, as in my case, the energy for the role of symbolic leader. Perhaps the symbolic monarch can be selected on merit from among the descendants of Confucius (there are more than three hundred thousand in China, mainly in Shandong Province). I could think of some who might fit the role. But I will end here, before I further alienate readers.

# NOTES

## Introduction

1. See Wang Zhimin and Eleni Karamalengou, eds., 稷下学宫与柏拉图学园：比较研究论集 [The Jixia Academy and Plato's Academy: A collection of comparative research] (Beijing: SDX Joint Publishing Company, 2021).

2. See William Kirby, *Empire of Ideas: Creating the Modern University from Germany to America to China* (Cambridge, Mass.: Harvard University Press, 2022), ch. 9. My own experience at Tsinghua suggests that internationalization has a long way to go: I was hired in 2004 and remained the only full-time foreign teacher in the Department of Philosophy until I left in 2017. In early 2022, the prestigious Renmin University in Beijing announced that it would no longer participate in international university rankings, which may reflect a somewhat worrisome countertrend to "de-internationalize" China's higher education system (https://www.weekinchina.com/2022/05/education-divide/?dm&utm_medium=email&utm_campaign=WiC585%2020%20May%202022%20Clients&utm_content=WiC585%2020%20May%202022%20Clients+CID_660d1e40354ace677892475cd884fcc7&utm_source=weeklyemail&utm_term=Education%20divide).

3. Shortly before I arrived in 2017, Shandong University had hired the distinguished University of Chicago scholar Yang Dali to start up a research institute in governance.

4. See https://journals.sagepub.com/doi/full/10.1177/1028315321990745 and https://link.springer.com/content/pdf/10.1007/BF03397011.pdf.

5. By "conservative," I mean that people in Shandong are unusually attached to Chinese traditional culture and less open to influences from the outside world compared with other parts of China. The dark side of Shandong-style conservatism is stronger attachment to patriarchal norms. For discussion, see Daniel A. Bell and Wang Pei, *Just Hierarchy: Why Social Hierarchies Matter in China and the Rest of the World* (Princeton, N.J.: Princeton University Press, 2020), pp. 1–6.

6. See Dingxin Zhao, *The Confucian-Legalist State: A New Theory of Chinese History* (Oxford: Oxford University Press, 2015).

7. See Guy S. Alitto, *The Last Confucian: Liang Shu-ming and the Chinese Dilemma of Modernity* (Berkeley: University of California Press, 1986).

8. See Daniel A. Bell and Thaddeus Metz, "Confucianism and Ubuntu: Reflections on a Dialogue between Chinese and African Traditions," *Journal of Chinese Philosophy* 38, no. s1 (2011): 78–95.

9. For an English translation of Jiang's works, see Jiang Qing, *A Confucian Constitutional Order: How China's Ancient Past Can Shape Its Political Future* (Princeton, N.J.: Princeton University Press, 2012). For an account of my visit to Jiang's academy, see https://www.dissentmagazine.org/online_articles/a-visit-to-a-confucian-academy.

10. See Bai Tongdong, *Against Political Equality: The Confucian Case* (Princeton, N.J.: Princeton University Press, 2019).

11. See http://citeseerx.ist.psu.edu/viewdoc/download?doi=10.1.1.733.6634&rep=rep1&type=pdf#page=968.

12. The journal *Culture, History, and Philosophy* received a significant boost when President Xi visited its editorial headquarters in Jinan, Shandong, in May 2021. Its English-language counterpart, the *Journal of Chinese Humanities*, is edited by another American émigré, Benjamin Hammer.

13. This paragraph draws on the preface to the paperback edition of my book *China's New Confucianism: Politics and Everyday Life in a Changing Society* (Princeton, N.J.: Princeton University Press, 2008).

14. The Confucian heritage is also prominent in museums and cultural sites about other former states in the Warring States era in the area that we now call Shandong. The Qi Dynasty Culture Museum in Zibo proudly discusses the Qi state's contribution to the Confucian tradition, and the Tengzhou museum highlights Mencius's passages about the tiny but plucky Teng state. The one exception is the Mozi Memorial Hall (also in Tengzhou), which explicitly casts Confucian contributions in a negative light in contrast to Mozi's ideals and inventions. My wife and I went to the Mozi Memorial Hall with an otherwise cool-headed descendant of Confucius, who was fuming after the visit.

15. By some stroke of bad luck, I often found myself seated under the quotation "When your parents are alive, do not travel far" (4.19), a reminder of the guilt I feel because I can't provide care for my elderly mother in Montreal (my sister provides the care).

16. See the excellent Discovery Channel documentary *Confucius: The Sage Who Shaped the East*: https://www.youtube.com/watch?v=qaFDr11g4Rg.

17. Anna Sun, *Confucianism as a World Religion: Contested Histories and Contemporary Realities* (Princeton, N.J.: Princeton University Press, 2013), pp. 90–91. For an empirically informed account of the Confucian revival, see Sebastien Billioud and

Joel Thoravel, *The Sage and the People: The Confucian Revival in China* (Oxford: Oxford University Press, 2015).

18. See my entry in the *Stanford Encyclopedia of Philosophy*: https://plato.stanford .edu/entries/communitarianism/.

19. Just as joining the World Trade Organization helped reformist forces in China to justify unpopular policies such as the sacking of millions of workers in state-owned enterprises, so increased U.S. antagonism helps the security apparatus to justify hard-line policies that are unpopular among reformist parts of the government. The main way external forces can "change China" is by providing an excuse for parts of the Chinese government to push through policies that would otherwise be difficult to implement.

20. As in China, public officials in the United States often feel freer to publicly counter dominant narratives after they retire. See, e.g., the insightful account of what's wrong with U.S.-China relations and how to fix it by Chas. W. Freeman Jr. (retired U.S. defense official, diplomat, and interpreter): https://peacediplomacy.org /2021/09/10/ipd-remarks-ambassador-chas-freeman-sino-american-split/. In the same vein, the former governor of California Jerry Brown condemns what he calls "Washington's crackpot realism," which obscures the reality that both countries must cooperate as well as compete (https://www.nybooks.com/articles/2022/03/24 /washingtons-crackpot-realism-jerry-brown/). See also the informed and balanced analysis of U.S.-China relations by Ken Lieberthal, who served in the Clinton administration as special assistant to the president for national security affairs and senior director for Asia on the U.S. National Security Council (https://www .thewirechina.com/2022/04/24/ken-lieberthal-on-washingtons-major-china -challenges/). The same is true of retired officials in other countries: See, e.g., the balanced account of U.S.-China relations by the former Australian prime minister Kevin Rudd, *The Avoidable War: The Dangers of a Catastrophic Conflict between the US and Xi Jinping's China* (New York: PublicAffairs, 2022).

21. I do not mean to imply that U.S. hostility to China is the only source of paranoia. The Legalist-inspired anti-corruption campaign drive has created many political enemies, and the leaders have good reasons to fear backlash from hundreds of thousands of purged cadres and their supporters. Now that the campaign seems to be winding down, such pressure may gradually diminish (see chapter 4).

22. To be more precise, hawkish forces in China do not threaten war with the United States unless the United States actively (or militarily) supports formal independence for Taiwan.

23. That said, China and the United States could go to war in East Asia, eventually spilling to warfare on or near American territory; see Graham Allison, *Destined for War: Can America and China Escape Thucydides's Trap?* (New York: Houghton Mifflin

Harcourt, 2017). For an even more pessimistic view, see John Mearscheimer (https://www.dw.com/en/chinas-rise-and-conflict-with-us/a-55026173). In contrast, Yan Xuetong, China's leading realist thinker, argues that China's aim is to become strong without going to war (https://www.foreignaffairs.com/articles/united-states/2021-06-22/becoming-strong).

24. https://www.washingtonpost.com/opinions/the-pentagon-is-using-china-as-an-excuse-for-huge-new-budgets/2021/03/18/848c8296-8824-11eb-8a8b-5cf82c3dffe4_story.html.

25. https://ash.harvard.edu/publications/understanding-ccp-resilience-surveying-chinese-public-opinion-through-time and https://www.edelman.com/sites/g/files/aatuss191/files/2022-01/2022%20Edelman%20Trust%20Barometer%20FINAL_Jan25.pdf.

26. https://themarket.ch/interview/chinas-leadership-is-prisoner-of-its-own-narrative-ld.6545.

27. Given the current repressive political environment (see chapter 8), this kind of confessional book, warts and all, is unlikely to get published in China. My own view is that more truthful accounts of the Chinese political system would be good for it—they would lend support to reformist forces who are both supporters and critics of the political system and who hope it evolves in a more humane direction—but no doubt I'm being politically naïve once again.

28. What's unusual about Pu Yi's confessions is that they were published in book form for the public. In post-revolutionary China, the closest approximation of type one confessions—expressions of moral wrongdoing from the perspective of a higher moral truth that allows for moral progress—tend to take place within groups of CCP members in the form of self-criticisms (自我批评) and mutual critiques (相互批评) that do not see the light of day in the public realm. To what extent such confessions are formulaic or insincere cannot be judged from the outside any more than we can judge the sincerity of confidential confessions told to Catholic priests.

## Chapter 1

1. Quoted in the *Australian*, September 2, 2007.

2. https://www.goodyardhairblog.com/how-did-old-ancient-dye-hair.html.

3. https://www.bbc.com/news/world-asia-china-21738733.

4. Quoted in ibid.

5. I'm following the Chinese usage here: we refer to "white hair" (白头发), not "gray hair," the more common usage in English. From a scientific point of view, both usages are misleading: "The hair is actually clear, not grey or white. This is due to lack of melanin and pigmentation in the hair follicles. It only appears grey or white by the

way light is reflected on them" (http://www.differencebetween.net/science/health/difference-between-grey-and-white-hair/).

6. Zheng Yongnian and Chen Gang, "China's Political Outlook: Xi Jinping as a Game Changer," *East Asian Policy* 7, no. 1 (2015): 5–15 (https://www.worldscientific.com/doi/abs/10.1142/S179393051500001X).

7. There are other exceptions to this political norm, such as Foreign Minister Wang Yi and Vice-Minister Liu He. But they are not part of the collective leadership and they often deal with foreigners, who may prefer the more "natural" look.

8. Quoted in https://edition.cnn.com/style/article/xi-jinping-gray-hair/index.html.

9. I use scare quotes around the term "natural" because it's possible that President Xi's hairstylist has perfected a method of dyeing hair black with bits of white so the outcome looks natural. I know of a dean in China who dyes his hair black with fashionable streaks of gray hair that look more "natural."

10. For more details, see chapter 3.

11. Note-taking does not always correspond to the content of what's being said. I'm too embarrassed to confess some of the things I wrote during those meetings.

12. My (ex) mother-in-law has been suffering from Alzheimer's disease for more than a decade and has progressively lost use of her mental faculties. A telling sign is that she no longer dyes her hair. For one miraculous day in early 2017, however, she recovered her old self. She woke up in a glorious mood with full use of her language faculties. She looked in the mirror and her first request was to dye her hair. We brought her to a hair stylist and it was one of the happiest days of her life. The next day, however, she succumbed again to the disease. I looked online for examples of Alzheimer's patients who made similar (temporary) recoveries and could not find any. It really was a miracle!

13. In Kazuo Ishiguro's novel *Klara and the Sun* (New York: Knopf, 2021), the otherwise plausible AI has the ability to detect people's precise age. I surmise that even advanced AIs would be fooled by a good dye job.

14. Elaine Scarry, *On Beauty and Being Just* (Princeton, N.J.: Princeton University Press, 2001).

15. I do not mean to imply that removing the prejudice against dyeing men's hair is sufficient to bring about equality between men and women. In the eighteenth century, well-to-do European men wore glorious wigs to cover up ugly or nonexistent hair and it was not viewed as a source of embarrassment. Even Jean-Jacques Rousseau, who otherwise disdained the world of appearances created by the arts and sciences that corrupted our original good nature, mentions that he started to wear a "round wig" after he had success with his prize-winning essay *Discourse on the Arts and Sciences* (Jean Jacques Rousseau, *The Confessions*, trans. J. M. Cohen [London:

Penguin Books, 1953], p. 339). His point is that he could wear a less fancy wig as an indication of the more "independent state" to which he aspired, but it's interesting that he still felt the need to wear a wig. My point is that even a society where men are vain enough to dye their hair won't be sufficient to bring about equality between men and women so long as other patriarchal values and structures remain in place. But it can help.

16. Gray hair is more prominent in Hong Kong, no doubt another legacy of British colonialism.

17. Rousseau, *The Confessions*, p. 17.

18. Ibid., pp. 50–51.

# Chapter 2

1. www.whitehouse.gov/briefing-room/speeches-remarks/2021/06/13 /remarks-by-president-biden-in-press-conference-2/.

2. I visited the Jixia Academy with three former students from Schwarzman College in July 2020, though all we could find was a sign with a cornfield in the background. In February 2022, archaeologists discovered the precise site of the Jixia Academy (https://www.scmp.com/news/people-culture/article/3170781 /archaeologists-discover-centre-greatest-chinese-philosophers), so it can plausibly be rebuilt as a site for tourist visits if not debates in political theory.

3. The name is even more misleading in Chinese: The literal translation of "统一战线" is "United War Front." I'm told that the department is considering changing the Chinese name to "团结部," which translates literally as "Solidarity Department."

4. See https://asiasociety.org/sites/default/files/2020-01/00_diamond-schell -chinas-influence-and-american-interests_REVISED.pdf and https://www .washingtonpost.com/opinions/2020/06/10/its-time-end-chinas-united-front -operations-inside-united-states/.

5. The buildings of the nearby Ocean University are more authentic imitations (if that's not an oxymoron) of German-style buildings from Qingdao's colonial era, but they were built more than two decades ago. Since then, the reaction against excessive "Westernization" in China has also called into question architecture that imitates Western models.

6. Tsinghua University ranks higher than Shandong University, but there is a kind of reverse affirmative action that makes it easier for relatively privileged students from Beijing to be admitted to Beijing-based universities. Shandong University is so competitive because the province has more than one hundred million people and it's the only leading university in the whole province. I've taught at both universities,

and my experience is that the students at both universities have similar academic ability, with the one difference that students at Tsinghua tend to have better English, which helps to explain why they typically do better on national university entrance examinations (which have an English component).

7. Surprisingly, perhaps, our campus does not have a statue of Confucius (the Jinan campus has a statue, as does the nearby Ocean University). Perhaps K. *shuji* felt that it would cross the line from public to private if he pushed for a statue of his great ancestor.

8. The sea off Shandong Province is closed to commercial fishing for environmental reasons from May to September, so seafood is more plentiful in the winter.

9. I later found out that K. *shuji* had expert knowledge of Marxist theory, and we had long discussions over dinner about Marx's ideal of communism, which reminded me of graduate days at Oxford when I studied Marxism with G. A. Cohen, the most distinguished Marxist theorist in the West. Unlike Oxford, however, debates in China seem more grounded in reality, given that the ruling organization is officially committed to Marxism. K. *shuji* was less optimistic than I am that material abundance produced by advanced machinery (including AI) in higher communism would change human nature for the better. I said a similar idea could be derived from Mencius's point that it's hard for people to be moral when they are striving for material necessities, but K. *shuji* was not persuaded. We converged on the point that, contra Marx, the state will not wither away in higher communism because it will be needed to ensure that AI serves people rather than the other way around. We also agreed that there would continue to be competition for the prestigious bureaucratic posts in higher communism, especially in Shandong Province, the most bureaucratic part of the world's most bureaucratic country. See chapter 7 for more details about the Communist comeback in China.

10. It was a more complicated process. K. *shuji* came to Beijing several times to persuade me and won my heart by appealing to my emotions. Tsinghua University sent two high-ranking administrators to Shandong University to ask K. *shuji* to let me stay at Tsinghua. I tried to leave Tsinghua, but it was difficult for complicated bureaucratic reasons (in China, it can be more difficult to divorce a university than to divorce a spouse). Tsinghua finally let me go after an alleged scandal that I will not recount here.

11. Some of these directives can be quite lengthy, and the *shuji* would sometimes read from documents for ten minutes or so, which really puts people to sleep. I asked a colleague: Why waste time like this? Is it because the documents are secret and cannot be distributed in advance? My colleague replied that nobody would read the documents if they were sent in advance.

12. See chapter 8.

13. Li Zhang, *Anxious China: Inner Revolution and Politics of Psychotherapy* (Oakland: University of California Press, 2020), pp. 6, 55–56.

14. I do not mean to imply that universities in the West necessarily work according to this academic ideal. There is no formal system of political censorship in Western universities, but informal norms of "political correctness" can influence hiring and tenure decisions regardless of academic merit. In China studies, for example, a professor who espouses positive or balanced views on the Chinese political system might experience job difficulties, and an academic who questions the dichotomy between "democratic" and "authoritarian" regimes might find it difficult to publish in prestigious Anglophone journals.

## Chapter 3

1. It's a bit odd that an official document titled "China: Democracy that Works" leads off with the claim that "the best way to evaluate whether a country's political system is democratic and efficient is to observe whether the succession of its leaders is orderly and in line with the law" (http://www.news.cn/english/2021-12/04/c_1310351231.htm). One would have expected a document aiming to defend Chinese-style democracy either not to mention or to bury the point that there is now no clear way of ensuring the succession of top leaders, with attendant risks of disorder.

2. The saying, ironically, was first put forward by the anti-Confucian (Daoist) thinker Zhuangzi ( 庄子·天下 ).

3. The label "dean" also helps to get things done. I once missed a WeChat message saying that I had to pay my heating bill. I was away for a few weeks, and when I returned to my apartment, it was freezing cold and I was informed by university housing staff that it was too late to pay and I'd have to go without heat for the whole winter. When I mentioned that I was dean of a faculty that researches the provision of public services, she became friendlier and referred me to her boss, who quickly solved the problem (they found a way to take my money).

4. I'm a Canadian citizen but the bank clerk thought I should be included in the American category. He finally agreed to put me in the non-American category when I became visibly upset.

5. Hierarchical worldviews in China that distinguish between the moral quality of people (素质 *suzhi*) and levels of civilization (文明程度 *wenming chengdu*) sound ridiculous when translated into contemporary English with its (formal) commitment to equality between people(s). The men's bathroom at Shandong University has the same slogan that's common above urinals in the rest of China: 上前一小步，文明一大步 (*shang qian yi xiao bu, wenming yi da bu*), which can be translated as "one small step forward, one big step in level of civilization."

6. My assistant lasted less than one year. Eventually, I discovered the way to secure an assistant: I could hire a second-year master's level student, since they have less course work and they experience less culture shock than new students do. The downside is that I have to train a new assistant every year.

7. A friend in Israel who had served as dean told me that he learned about problems in his faculty by strolling the halls, bumping into junior teachers, and chatting with them. The problem in our faculty is that senior leaders (including myself) are all on one floor and it would seem odd (or inappropriate) if I were to randomly stroll the halls of the junior faculty.

8. I learned later that, before going into academia, our executive vice-dean had founded a thriving restaurant business in Jinan with twelve hundred employees, which no doubt helps to explain his ability to manage others in a large university setting (I have difficulty managing myself, never mind other people).

9. My suggestions were not all warmly welcomed. I tried to persuade our faculty to hire a well-known professor famous for his "conversion" from libertarianism to Confucianism. He had recently joined our university (I had helped to persuade him to join us) and he was initially based at a research institute in Jinan. I hoped he'd join our faculty in Qingdao. There was a distinct lack of enthusiasm from fellow leaders, and the professor was eventually poached by a leading university in Beijing.

10. It was a complicated process because a leader at his university did not want to let him go, but things changed for the better (from my perspective) when the leader became ensnared in the anti-corruption campaign.

11. I also received great help from one of my former doctoral students from Tsinghua University, who did a thesis on political meritocracy. She was hired at Shandong University and launched an informal lunchtime seminar for graduate students and professors that came to be known as the "稷下工作坊" (Jixia workshop), named after the famous Warring States–period Jixia Academy, where great political thinkers discussed their ideas.

12. It is common for drunken males to hold hands in Shandong. In my first year, however, I was not always sure of the boundaries of physical affection. I once kissed a visiting *shuji* on the cheek and immediately realized it was a *faux pas*. Holding hands is fine, but "tough men from Shandong" (山东大汉) do not kiss.

13. When I'm asked what I learned as dean, I tell the joke that at the start I had no idea when to intervene and when not to intervene and eventually learned that I should not intervene 98 percent of the time. But the truth is that I could have intervened more if I had more energy for the job.

14. Daniel A. Bell, *The China Model: Political Meritocracy and the Limits of Democracy* (Princeton, N.J.: Princeton University Press, 2015), ch. 2.

15. This point would not surprise students of Chinese history. Chen Hongmou, for example, was the most celebrated administrator in eighteenth-century China, but what really set him apart was his astonishing energy level. As Chen's biographer puts it, "Chen was hardly an original thinker, nor did his style of administration differ substantially from that of his most capable colleagues, but his energy level and his thoroughness in addressing the needs of his various jurisdictions was nothing short of astounding" (William T. Rowe, *Saving the World: Chen Hongmou and Elite Consciousness in Eighteenth-Century China* [Stanford, Calif.: Stanford University Press, 2001], p. 2; see also p. 449).

16. David Shambaugh, "The Coming Chinese Crackup," *Wall Street Journal*, March 6, 2015.

17. https://www.cambridge.org/core/journals/american-political-science -review/article/abs/getting-ahead-in-the-communist-party-explaining-the -advancement-of-central-committee-members-in-china/B22B6ACD187AD664C CCD6497E6A165BE.

18. I do not mean to deny that less savory personality traits inconsistent with the ideal of political meritocracy, such as the willingness to promote friends who are not qualified and to purge political rivals, may also play a role in explaining who gets to the top and stays there. For an empirically informed argument that leaders such as Mao with unconstrained dictatorial power replace experienced and well-connected senior officials with less-qualified and politically tainted officials, see Victor Shih, *Coalitions of the Weak: Elite Politics in China from Mao's Stratagem to the Rise of Xi* (Cambridge: Cambridge University Press, 2022).

19. *The Analects of Confucius*, 13.15. Here and throughout, the translation is the author's unless indicated otherwise.

20. Jude Blanchette, "Xi Jinping's Faltering Foreign Policy," *Foreign Affairs*, March 16, 2022 (https://www.foreignaffairs.com/articles/china/2022-03-16/xi -jinpings-faltering-foreign-policy). Such claims are highly speculative: No one out-side the closed circle of top political leaders knows whether anyone dares to stand up to Xi's proposals.

21. https://www.scmp.com/news/china/politics/article/3159720/xi-jinping -tells-chinas-writers-and-artists-practise-morality.

22. So we know, for example, that the administrator Chen Hongmou was granted an audience with Emperor Yongzhen and he argued against the Emperor's proposal that corrupt local elites should publicly confess their misdeeds (on the grounds that this would undermine social order and it was better to issue a blanket pardon for past misdeeds and tighten controls in the future). Yongzhen was eventually persuaded by Chen's proposal and praised his "straightforward way of addressing a superior" in defense of the public interest (Rowe, *Saving the World*, p. 51).

## Chapter 4

1. I borrow this term from the political theorist Jane Mansbridge, who argued that it's difficult, if not impossible, to combat corruption without such "islands of probity" that can set good models for improvement (private conversation).

2. Cited in Ren Jianming and Du Zhizhou, "Institutionalized Corruption: Power Overconcentration of the First-in-Command in China," *Crime, Law and Social Change* 49, no. 1 (February 2008): 47.

3. The next two paragraphs draw on Bell and Wang, *Just Hierarchy*, pp. 81–84.

4. For an argument that anti-corruption efforts in non-democracies are often successful if a powerful leader has a relatively free hand to enact and enforce measures curbing government wrongdoing, see Christopher Carothers, *Corruption Control in Authoritarian Regimes: Lessons from East Asia* (Cambridge: Cambridge University Press, 2022), esp. ch. 6 (on the case of Xi).

5. For an empirically informed argument that the anti-corruption drive has a deterrent effect that lowers the average ability of newly recruited bureaucrats, see https://www.cambridge.org/core/journals/british-journal-of-political-science /article/price-of-probity-anticorruption-and-adverse-selection-in-the-chinese -bureaucracy/5CF35E3428FEE88814270F861360D3B8.

6. The need to raise salaries in order to minimize corruption was repeatedly emphasized by reformers in imperial China. As early as the second century, the philosopher Cui Shi proposed that the salaries of public officials should be increased by at least 50 percent (Etienne Balazs, *Chinese Civilization and Bureaucracy: Variations on a Theme*, trans. H. M. Wright [New Haven, Conn.: Yale University Press, 1964], p. 213). I did raise the possibility of increasing salaries in an informal meeting with a leader of the Organization Department, and he told me that they plan to do so eventually but it would be bad optics if they do too much too soon.

7. I would like to thank *American Affairs* for permission to draw on my essay "China's Anti-corruption Campaign and the Challenges of Political Meritocracy," *American Affairs* 4, no. 2 (Summer 2020): 198–211.

## Chapter 5

1. Edward Slingerland, *Drunk: How We Sipped, Danced, and Stumbled Our Way to Civilization* (New York: Little, Brown Spark, 2021), p. 115.

2. Liu Yaoding, "不喝酒, 如何在山东的酒桌上活下来," [If you don't drink alcohol, how can you survive Shandong's drinking tables], June 20, 2018, https:// baijiahao.baidu.com/s?id=1604692088818172035&wfr=spider&for=pc.

3. For a detailed account and defense of such hierarchical drinking rituals, see the opening of my book co-authored with Wang Pei, *Just Hierarchy*.

4. https://www.cnbc.com/2021/08/09/alibaba-fires-manager-accused-of -sexual-assault-ceo-calls-for-change.html.

5. Here and elsewhere, I've drawn on the translations Eric L. Hutton, *Xunzi: The Complete Text* (Princeton, N.J.: Princeton University Press, 2014), and John Knoblock, *Xunzi, I and II* [with original Chinese and modern Chinese side by side] (Changsha: Hunan Renmin Chubanshe, 1999). I've adapted these translations if need be; for example, I've translated "王 *wang*" as "humane king" rather than simply "king" because Xunzi uses this term to refer to an ideal ruler who pursues humane policies for the people.

6. Rituals per se are not sufficient. They often need to be accompanied by music, which helps to trigger an emotional response and leads to a sense of community and mutual care among participants. Xunzi devotes a whole chapter to the moral and political effects of music, and still today, the Chinese word "ritual" (礼) is often followed by the word for "music" (乐), as though the two ideas are inseparable. Xunzi also argues for extensive and life-long reading of great works to enhance the mind, which, he says, can produce long-term transformations of human nature for the better.

7. For more details, see my book *China's New Confucianism*, pp. 39–43.

8. This discussion draws on Daniel Bell, "China's Corruption Clampdown Risks Policy Paralysis," *Financial Times*, May 2, 2017.

9. See https://www.sciencedirect.com/science/article/pii/S0033350616304139 and Wang Qian and Zhang Yan, "Drunken Driving Crashes, Injuries Declining," *China Daily*, October 10, 2014.

10. A similar story of "先礼后兵 *xianli houbing*" can be told of those who ignored speed limits. The educational efforts in driving schools and elsewhere to make drivers obey the rules of the road had little effect. The government then decided to use traffic cameras that fined drivers, with little room for discretion. That eventually worked to change driving practices. Today, the cameras have less effect because almost every car has a GPS (导航) that warns drivers of the presence of cameras, but still, most drivers have internalized the need to obey speed limits without being forced to do so. The point here is not that harsh laws per se can transform attitudes and actions. The fear of harsh punishment in the short term can help to transform inner morality in the long term only if the initial fear of punishment builds on a commonly held social value that is already internalized by means of education and informal rituals (people knew that drunk driving and speeding were bad, but such norms affected behavior only after they were backed up with harsh punishments for violations). Regarding other rules of the road, there is still need for progress. The government carries out public campaigns to promote civility by means of signs on

major roads with the characters "礼让 *li rang*," which can be translated as "ritual and deference." It's still quite rare, however, for drivers to show civility by letting pedestrians proceed first in cases of conflict: The powerful cars usually prevail and pedestrian crosswalks have little effect. Once the government issues strict fines for incivility, it may help to improve things, and once civility becomes second nature, the government will no longer need to rigorously enforce the law. I do not mean to imply that such processes are unique to China. In Montreal (my home town), crosswalks had little effect when I was a kid. Rude drivers were tamed by harsh fines and now cars generally defer to pedestrians without being forced to do so.

11. For another story with my (ex) father-in-law, see https://www.dissentmagazine.org/online_articles/the-last-visitor. At the time (2009), I wrote that he is one of the few true communists left in China, but little did I anticipate the communist comeback (see chapter 7).

## Chapter 6

1. One of the ironies of history is that the Kong family shows that bloodlines still matter. Kongzi's descendants had special privileges in imperial China. Today, they proudly partake of the world's oldest family tree and they are among the most committed and effective carriers of the Confucian tradition both inside and outside China. See https://www.youtube.com/watch?v=qaFDr11g4Rg.

2. Such impressions have a long history: John Locke (1695) referred disparagingly to the "incoherent apothegms of Confucius" in contrast to the "reasonableness of Christianity" (see excerpt in *Portraits of Confucius: The Reception of Confucianism from 1560 to 1960*, ed. Kevin Delapp [London: Bloomsbury Academic, 2022], pp. 193–195).

3. A helpful guide is Annping Chin's *The Authentic Confucius: A Life of Thought and Politics* (New York: Scribner, 2007), ch. 3.

4. The ideal may be appropriate for classes in higher education that involve teaching the Confucian virtues and the humanities more generally, but teaching young children and other disciplines (e.g., science classes with labs) may require different kinds of classrooms. That said, my experience teaching children of migrant workers in Beijing with my son Julien shows the value of a Confucian-inspired approach to teaching young children as well (see https://digitalcommons.unl.edu/cgi/viewcontent.cgi?article=1593&context=chinabeatarchive).

5. Needless to say, this kind of teaching is very time intensive. The ideal Confucian teacher teaches full time and can say goodbye to research. No wonder Confucius didn't have time to write his own ideas!

6. The liquor is more famous for its implicit invocation of the Confucian tradition than for its taste. I once purchased a bottle of Kong Mansion liquor at Qufu's train

station that was designed to look like a bamboo scroll of the *Analects of Confucius* (the bottle was hidden inside the text).

7. As U.S.-China relations worsened, the U.S. government barred graduates of West Point and other leading military academies from the Schwarzman program, presumably on the assumption that greater understanding of China might lead to more sympathy for the country. This is regrettable, in my view, both because such educational exchanges can help to reduce conflict and because Schwarzman scholars with military backgrounds can learn from some of China's ideas and practices to the benefit of the United States (see, e.g., Regina Parker's argument that Chinese-style military training for university students can and should be implemented in the United States: https://www.huffpost.com/entry/learning-from-communist-china_b_57fd794fe4b0210c1faea8a9).

8. If there's a complaint embedded in these remarks, it's not just because our course was downgraded. The program aims to promote better understanding of China, and my view is that students can't understand China without understanding key themes in Chinese history and culture. I repeatedly argued, without success, for more courses (besides our own) on pre-twentieth-century China.

9. I wasn't just flattering my local hosts. Chin-shing Huang contends that the arguments against Xunzi's enshrinement were largely unfair. If the two main standards for enshrinement are still valid—"the candidate's importance to the development of Confucian learning and his current relevance"—then there is a good case for the (re)enshrinement of Xunzi (Huang, *Confucianism and Sacred Space: The Confucius Temple from Imperial China to Today*, trans. Jonathan Chin with Chin-shing Huang [New York: Columbia University Press, 2020], p. 168).

10. See Han Feizi's critique of the "five vermin," including scholars who "cast doubt upon the laws of the state and cause the ruler to be of two minds." Han Feizi's advice to rulers is to "wipe out such vermin" (http://afe.easia.columbia.edu/ps/cup/hanfei_five_vermin.pdf).

## Chapter 7

1. Bell, *China's New Confucianism*, ch. 1.

2. https://www.marxists.org/archive/marx/works/1875/gotha/index.htm.

3. https://www.guancha.cn/LvDeWen/2021_09_14_607005.shtml.

4. See, e.g., https://www.nytimes.com/2022/01/05/technology/china-tech-internet-crackdown-layoffs.html and https://www.ft.com/content/e4df19e8-7247-4086-9f86-5364df06c145.

5. I do not mean to imply that everything the CCP does conforms to Marxist ideals. Marx would not have endorsed the clampdowns on freedom of speech and social criticism.

6. I visited Professor Z.'s apartment in 2016 to show my respect. I was surprised by his genuine commitment to Marxism and, even then, I thought that he was on the wrong side of history. He passed away in 2018, I regret to report. Today, I realize that I may have been on the wrong side of history, though I still think that socialism is not a science.

7. https://www.nytimes.com/live/2021/11/11/world/china-xi-jinping-cpc.

8. The next three paragraphs draw on Bell and Wang, *Just Hierarchy*, pp. 180–182.

9. http://english.www.gov.cn/news/top_news/2017/09/27/content _281475888488000.htm#:~:text=The%20realization%20of%20communism%20 is,as%20its%20guide%20to%20action.

10. See Haig Patapan and Wang Yi, "The Hidden Ruler: Wang Huning and the Making of Contemporary China," *Journal of Contemporary China*, October 2017, p. 9.

11. Quoted in https://asia.nikkei.com/Spotlight/Comment/Xi-Jinping-points -China-to-Communist-Revolution-2.0.

12. On Marx's distinction between lower and higher communism, see https:// www.marxists.org/archive/marx/works/1875/gotha/.

13. Quoted in Daniel Guérin, *Anarchism: From Theory to Practice* (New York: Monthly Review Press, 1970), pp. 25–26.

14. https://www.marxists.org/archive/marx/works/1874/04/bakunin-notes .htm.

15. David Stasavage, *The Decline and Rise of Democracy: A Global History from Antiquity to Today* (Princeton, N.J.: Princeton University Press, 2020).

16. Willy Wo-Lap Lam, "Beijing Harnesses Big Data and AI to Perfect the Police State," Jamestown Foundation, July 21, 2017.

17. https://www.marxists.org/archive/marx/works/1845/german-ideology /ch01a.htm.

18. See Feng Xiang, "我是阿尔法— 论人际关系伦理" [On human-computer ethics], *Wenhua zongheng* 12 (2017): 128–139.

19. https://thenewobjectivity.com/pdf/marx.pdf.

20. Nick Bostrom, *Superintelligence: Paths, Dangers, Strategies* (Oxford: Oxford University Press, 2014).

21. For a more developed argument, see Bell and Wang, *Just Hierarchy*, ch. 5.

22. For an argument that Legalist-style coercion was necessary (but not suffi-cient) to deal with Covid in China, see Daniel A. Bell and Wang Pei, "Just Hierarchy," *American Purpose*, August 4, 2021 (https://www.americanpurpose.com/articles/just -hierarchy/).

23. David J. Chalmers, *Reality +: Virtual Worlds and the Problems of Philosophy* (New York: Norton, 2022).

24. Lenin's idea of a vanguard party with proletarian consciousness was meant for an industrial society in times of revolutionary upheaval, so the lessons for today are far from clear.

25. https://ctext.org/liji/li-yun.

## Chapter 8

1. https://www.bartleby.com/130/1.html.

2. https://journals.sagepub.com/doi/10.1177/0306422015591436?icid=int.sj-abstract.similar-articles.3.

3. See chapter 9 for more details.

4. At Tsinghua University, I did run into political trouble because of a comment I wrote in the *Financial Times* suggesting that the CCP change its name (I made a similar point in an academic book, but politically sensitive points are of greater concern when they are published in popular media). The leader invited me to his office and offered to serve me tea. I said, "No thanks, I'd rather have coffee." I knew I was in trouble when he insisted on serving me tea, code for a session of political scolding. The problem is that the comment was (mis)translated into Chinese to suggest that I favored overthrowing the CCP. I explained the mistranslation and the leader was satisfied with my explanation. He recommended that the next time, I should supervise a translation and get it out there before the mistranslations. It seemed like a reasonable suggestion, but perhaps he was overestimating the amount of control I have over the process of public dissemination of information in an age of social media.

5. It's been changing for the worse the past few years. Even English-language academic works are banned from classrooms if they infringe on sensitive topics—e.g., if the author uses the word "country" to describe Taiwan.

6. https://www.xuetangx.com/course/sdu01011004962intl/7733555?channel=home_course_ad.

7. To encourage students to speak up (students from Shandong are hard-working but unusually shy and polite, perhaps as a legacy of the Confucian culture), I break them up into groups of three and let one student represent the group's views. That way, they feel freer to say what they think without taking direct responsibility for what they say. Eventually, diverse viewpoints and clear differences emerge and then I call on individual students to elaborate contrasting viewpoints.

8. That being said, it is not so easy to teach contemporary interpretations of Marxism that differ from government-approved views, especially if they bear on the Chinese political context. I was forbidden to use my book *Just Hierarchy* (co-authored with Wang Pei) in a graduate seminar on the grounds that we criticize misuses of Marxism in China. Ironically, the same book has been criticized by Western critics

for being too "pro-CCP" (see the new preface for the paperback of *Just Hierarchy* published in 2022).

9. There are some positive counter-trends: Social scientific work on environmental problems that may have been off limits in the past is often welcomed by the authorities today, if only because environmental progress is now a governmental priority and "they" know that academic research can help with the political cause.

10. One of my colleagues noted a sophisticated form of censorship. A few years ago, he had translated a huge book on a recent Chinese leader by a famous American academic. He asked me to guess which part of his Chinese translation had been censored. I guessed the part about the June 4, 1989, killings in Beijing. He said yes, but that's not the main part. Only those with a good understanding of Chinese politics could guess right, he added: It's the index; they just want to make it harder for people to find what has been said about whom.

11. See chapter 4.

12. I am grateful to Song Bing, who worked tirelessly to proofread the book and help to get it through the censors by means of such strategies.

13. https://www.jstor.org/stable/24027184.

14. https://www.scmp.com/comment/opinion/article/3051402/coronavirus-holds-mirror-chinas-problems-and-nation-will-be-better.

15. https://www.nytimes.com/2015/04/17/opinion/teaching-western-values-in-china.html.

16. If China does relax censorship in society at large and academia in particular, it will show its commitment to political meritocracy, similar to the case of Singapore. As John Stuart Mill argued in *On Liberty*, freedom of speech allows for the critique of mistaken ideas and the expression of new and better ideas and ways of life as well as for the range of choice that enables us to identify and empower the "wise and noble" among us. Freedom of speech matters because it helps to identify not just *what* is important but also *who* is important. If censorship and media controls are increasingly used to enforce the rules and maintain ideological orthodoxy, the Chinese government will show its commitment to a Legalist autocratic tradition that values stability over social progress and adaptation to new circumstances. There may be a "meritocratic" case for censorship and strong social control if relatively well-informed elites agree on the political priority and the need to select leaders who can deliver the goods (for example, there was widespread agreement among elites in Singapore in the 1960s and 1970s and China in the 1970s and 1980s that poverty alleviation should be the priority and that political leaders should promote economic growth as the best means of enriching the people, and there wasn't much of a need to debate alternatives). But increased censorship of a highly educated and diverse population is a recipe for long-term disaster, particularly in a world of fast technological change and unpredictable global shocks that constantly require new thinking,

experimentation, and ways of dealing with unexpected challenges. The idea that we need freedom of speech to expose wrongdoing and put forward new and better ideas for policy making was also articulated by Confucius himself, who said that "if what a ruler says is not good and no one opposes him" is perhaps the one saying that can cause a state to perish (13.15). Such sayings were not mere theory: In the Tang and the Southern Song, perhaps the most vibrant dynasties in Chinese imperial history, there was substantial space for political criticism and the exploration of alternative views outside of official orthodoxy and relatively open and fair ways of selecting political leaders from diverse social and ethnic groups (compared to other periods in imperial history).

17. https://www.theguardian.com/commentisfree/2008/apr/02/badmouthing beijing.

18. Bell, *China's New Confucianism*, p. 8.

19. See the introduction to this book.

20. The next two paragraphs draw on my essay "Demonizing China: A Diagnosis with No Cure in Sight," in *East-West Reflections on Demonization: North Korea Now, China Next?*, eds. Geir Helgesen and Rachel Harrison (Copenhagen: NIAS Press, 2020), pp. 230–232.

21. Peter Drahos, *Survival Governance: Energy and Climate in the Chinese Century* (Oxford: Oxford University Press, 2021).

22. See Bell and Wang, *Just Hierarchy*, ch. 5.

23. That said, the Biden administration did succeed in passing an important bill aiming to counter climate change (https://www.nytimes.com/2022/08/07/us/politics/climate-tax-bill-passes-senate.html?action=click&module=RelatedLinks&pgtype=Article).

24. For more systematic argumentation, see my book *The China Model* and Bell and Wang, *Just Hierarchy*, ch. 2.

25. See, e.g., the comments section of https://www.youtube.com/watch?v=5C1mpNwFj8w. "五毛 *wu mao*" (literally, fifty cents) is a pejorative term referring to Internet trolls who are allegedly paid fifty cents per pro-CCP comment. I still think of myself as an independent scholar and write exactly what I think, but it's true that I've "gone native" in the sense that my academic work has often been informed by my experience living and teaching in mainland China. For example, I was inspired to write on the theme of political meritocracy by my experience at Tsinghua University, which trains many of China's future leaders and where my colleagues tended to argue about which virtues and abilities are important for public officials and how to assess those virtues and abilities. Had I stayed in the West—where there is a strong societal consensus that one-person, one-vote is the only morally legitimate way to select political leaders, and all other political systems are (bad) authoritarian regimes—it is highly unlikely I would have written on the topic of political meritocracy in China.

26. https://www.ft.com/content/903d37ac-2a63-11e2-a137-00144feabdc0.

27. China's political censors for the Chinese translation were not fooled: As mentioned, they submitted the longest list of requests for cuts my editor had ever seen.

28. https://www.wsj.com/articles/can-anyone-be-chinese-1500045078.

29. I'm frequently asked to appear on Chinese media, but I only accept offers that are not open to political misuses and where I have control over the final product. Here too, however, things sometimes go wrong at the end, when senior censors overrule editors who had made promises not to cut. In the most recent case, I did a TEDx talk on political meritocracy. I made sure to argue that there is a large gap between the ideal and the reality and that more democracy and free speech are necessary to minimize that gap. I told the organizers that my talk would be credible to a foreign audience only if they kept the critical parts and that I'd agree to have it distributed only if they did not delete them. Most critical parts were deleted anyway and it was distributed on TEDx. A couple of weeks later, it had more than fifty thousand hits but the talk was deleted by TEDx (it felt more than a bit odd to be censored on both ends). I wrote to TED to ask why but never received a response. In the unlikely event that the reader is interested in the cut version of my talk, the link is https://pan.baidu.com/s/1mdjAHiSIEgc3_QYL9zpmrA.

30. In November 2021, the United States and China agreed to ease restrictions on journalists, one of the few positive signs of cooperation between the two great powers.

31. https://www.scmp.com/comment/opinion/article/3127609/improve-chinas-image-globally-welcome-foreigners-and-let-them-be.

32. From an author's point of view, another advantage of dealing with the Chinese media is that authors are usually consulted regarding headlines and can exercise veto power over ones they don't like.

# Chapter 9

1. David Shambaugh, *China's Communist Party: Atrophy and Adaptation* (Berkeley: University of California Press, 2008).

2. My impression is that such questions are mainly opportunities for enemies or rivals to cast doubt on the candidates. Open or formal questioning of political loyalty is equivalent to a "nuclear bomb," I was told by a confidant, meaning that it should never be used in academia except as a last resort.

3. There is a general trend toward empowerment of party secretaries in Chinese universities (as social life has become more politicized since President Xi assumed power). But in our case, it happened because our super-talented executive vice-dean was burdened with two jobs (see chapter 3) and somebody had to help with some tasks. At the start, there was speculation that I might step in, but I lacked the energy

(and perhaps the ability) to do so. Our party secretary gradually took on more of a leadership role, which turned out quite well because he is well-liked and fair-minded (not to mention hard-working).

4. In my acceptance speech to the leaders of the new collective leadership committee, I urged everyone to do their work well since, I said jokingly, I'd be responsible if things went wrong. Deep in my heart, however, I knew that a more accurate description of my role would be "not responsible for any administration of the faculty; only responsible for symbolic leadership." See chapter 11 for more details.

5. We tell this story in Bell and Wang, *Just Hierarchy*, pp. 76–77, but it's too good not to repeat here.

6. The founding father of our faculty, Professor Z. (now deceased), told me that the two main traits of CCP members should be (1) a willingness to die, and (2) an ability to keep secrets. I didn't reply, but if I had I would have said that surely it depends on the context, with different traits important for different kinds of public officials. For example, the first trait might be relevant for soldiers and the second for spies. Now I'd add that the ability to keep secrets may also be important for members of the Organization Department.

7. The *gaokao* is widely regarded as the most meritocratic and least corrupt institution in the Chinese political system, though it penalizes underprivileged young people in poor rural areas who do not have access to good teachers and preparatory schools. See Zachary M. Howlett, *Meritocracy and Its Discontents: Anxiety and the National College Entrance Exam in China* (Ithaca, N.Y.: Cornell University Press, 2021).

8. We had to make an exception in April 2022 because students could not come to campus for examinations due to Covid restrictions. We organized relatively formal day-long oral examinations via the Internet and the examiners (including myself) had to submit our phones to an administrator during the examination process to ensure that our attention would be focused on what we were supposed to be doing (it was the closest I'd come to my never-realized plan at the start of my deanship for a phone-free day on campus).

9. In Chinese universities, only senior professors (博导) have the right to supervise doctoral students. They also have the privilege of retiring five years later than professors without this title.

10. Our university is particularly wary of any procedures that seem to allow subjective factors to influence promotions precisely because, I speculate, the Confucian-influenced Shandong culture so strongly emphasizes warm and caring social relations and "讲义气," which we can roughly translate as a willingness to sacrifice for brotherly friends (another translation might be "bro justice"). Hence, there is a need to put in place rigid measures to prevent the influence of "subjective" factors that may not be

necessary in other parts of China (such as Shanghai), where social relations tend to be more instrumental and people more respectful of rules and procedures. That said, there may be ways to ensure more impartial academic judgments that include subjective assessments of the content of research. One possibility, similar to the practice in Hong Kong's universities, is for candidates considered for promotion to submit what they consider three of their best publications over the previous five years to be assessed by a small, anonymous committee of academics in the relevant field from different universities.

11. I've heard of, but not personally witnessed, another problem: discrimination against female academics because of the sexist assumption that they are more devoted to the family than the workplace. What's clear is that there is insufficient support such as day care facilities for parents with young children, which tends to have a more negative impact on female academics who are often more burdened with housework and family duties. And formal discrimination persists in the sense that female academics (like other public officials in China) must retire five years earlier than their male counterparts (fifty-five for most female professors, sixty for "PhD supervisors" 博导).

12. How many Western academics can write high-quality works in more than one language? It's also a self-criticism: I can write emails and short works in Chinese but have yet to attempt to write an academic article in Chinese.

13. We have an even more impressive plan to develop a world-class faculty by the year 2035. Here, too, we are in competition with other faculties in political science and public administration in mainland Chinese universities, given the limited number of top "grades." We also have a (less detailed) plan for 2050 that further consolidates our world-class status. I dearly hope that our faculty continues to make progress. But I'd be more than pleasantly surprised if we can vault beyond faculties in political science and public administration at other universities in China and the rest of the world. Let me borrow a joke I heard from one of our professors: Our plans will be fully realized at the same time that the Chinese male soccer team wins the World Cup.

14. Professors are incentivized by means of large cash bonuses for articles published in leading academic journals. But the pressure to publish and apply for government research grants can be psychologically overwhelming, especially for younger professors.

15. In contrast, professors in Western universities tend to get rewarded primarily for highly specialized research regardless of social impact, and universities are often criticized for being elite institutions detached from the needs of ordinary citizens. It might not be a bad idea if academics were partly evaluated by their commitment to the public interest, however hard it may be to assess such contributions. There may be something to learn from the Chinese experience in this respect.

## Chapter 10

1. https://www.scmp.com/news/china/diplomacy/article/3135672/xi-jinping-wants-isolated-china-make-friends-and-win-over.

2. https://china.huanqiu.com/article/43MyYRilpCV.

3. Shanghai is perhaps the "capital of cuteness" in China: In the early days of the harsh two-month lockdown in April and May 2022, some Shanghainese lined up for Covid testing in cute animal costumes. By the end of the lockdown, however, the lighthearted spirit of Shanghainese-style cuteness had been killed off, and one can only hope that it will be recovered in the future.

4. For more details, see Bell and Wang, *Just Hierarchy*, pp. 102–104.

5. https://edition.cnn.com/2018/11/08/china/gavin-meme-kid-china-intl/index.html.

6. https://journals.plos.org/plosone/article?id=10.1371/journal.pone.0046362.

7. Simon May, *The Power of Cute* (Princeton, N.J.: Princeton University Press, 2019), p. 9.

8. This section draws on Daniel A. Bell and Wang Pei, "How a Cute Baby Elephant Sheds Light on China's Quest for Soft Power," *South China Morning Post*, June 24, 2021.

9. See, e.g., https://www.nytimes.com/2021/06/03/world/asia/china-elephants.html; https://www.bbc.co.uk/newsround/57414955; https://edition.cnn.com/2021/06/09/china/elephants-china-yunnan-intl-hnk/index.html.

10. https://www.scmp.com/news/people-culture/trending-china/article/3135726/after-500km-journey-herd-15-elephants-closing.

11. See https://nypost.com/2021/06/10/drone-captures-elephant-herds-nap-after-300-plus-mile-trek/.

12. http://www.xinhuanet.com/english/2021-06/12/c_1310004751.htm.

13. I particularly empathized with the drunken elephants, who supposedly fell asleep after helping themselves to some corn wine from a villager's home, though I regret to report the story may be apocryphal (https://www.thatsmags.com/china/post/30902/this-drunk-elephants-in-yunnan-story-is-what-we-need-right-now).

14. "有人竟花1万给猫拉了双眼皮," [Believe it or not, some people spend 10,000 rmb on double-eyelids for cats], *Guancha Syndicate*, February 27, 2019.

15. John Stuart Mill, *On Liberty* (https://www.gutenberg.org/files/34901/34901-h/34901-h.htm).

16. There were strong expressions of dissatisfaction during the inhumane two-month lockdown of Shanghai in early 2022, but if the government had tried to impose a similar lockdown in Beijing, it might have had a revolution on its hands.

17. See https://www.scmp.com/abacus/culture/article/3029492/how-properly-use-three-popular-emoji-chinese-social-media.

18. Max Weber's essay "Politics as a Vocation" famously argued that the good politician must be guided by an "ethic of responsibility" that may entail the use of morally dubious means to get good results. Weber's distinction between the political leader who decides and the civil servant who implements, however, is context specific. In imperial China, there were not separate tracks for political officials and civil servants, and the same is true in contemporary China. See the discussion in my book *The China Model*, pp. 75–78. All those who serve the public are officials who are supposed to make hard decisions and accept responsibility for those decisions, though, of course, the level of power and responsibility increases at higher levels of government.

19. See Michael Marmot, "Spike by Jeremy Farrar with Anjana Ahuja—Ignoring the Science," *Financial Times*, July 28, 2021. He was also exposed for ignoring Covid-prevention regulations that his government imposed on the rest of the population.

20. Such considerations help to explain (but do not justify) why "cute" images of President Xi juxtaposed with Winnie the Pooh are censored in China (https://www.theguardian.com/world/2018/aug/07/china-bans-winnie-the-pooh-film-to-stop-comparisons-to-president-xi). It's not just that such images can be used to mock President Xi. Even if such images are used in a sympathetic way to communicate cuteness, they undermine the authority and dignity of a political leader who needs to make hard decisions for the common good.

21. Rarely does not mean never. I did sometimes help colleagues; most recently, I did my best to help colleagues stuck abroad due to Covid restrictions to return to China. Still, I did less other-regarding work than other leaders in my faculty, and in that sense, I failed to be a responsible dean.

22. See chapter 9 for more details. I should add that casting doubt on the value of such academic ranking systems in the grand scheme of the universe is not meant to criticize such systems in principle. We do need some sort of semi-objective system to rank academics competing for a limited number of spots.

23. Private conversation with Daniel Bell. At the official ceremony that conferred my deanship, hosted by the university president, I was introduced as a sociologist. The label stuck in official university documents and I never asked for a correction, in the hope that, as the real Daniel Bell put it, "a Chinese scholar in the future may be astounded by the discovery of the incredible longevity of a Daniel Bell with over ninety years of productivity" (quoted from faxed letter sent in 1993: see my obituary for Daniel Bell, https://www.dissentmagazine.org/online_articles/remembering-daniel-bell#bell).

## Chapter 11

1. See Jiang, *Confucian Constitutional Order*, ch. 3.

2. Ironically, Perry Link criticized an op-ed in the *New York Times* penned by Jiang Qing and me, saying, "there is nothing in it that the Standing Committee in Beijing would not like" (https://www.nytimes.com/2012/07/14/opinion/how-to-govern -china.html), which is a bit odd, given that any defense of symbolic monarchy would face the wrath of the censors in contemporary China.

3. https://www.statista.com/statistics/863893/support-for-the-monarchy-in -britain-by-age/.

4. https://www.rcinet.ca/en/2021/03/17/new-poll-suggests-support-of -monarchy-in-canada-continues-to-diminish/.

5. James Hankins, *Political Meritocracy in Renaissance Italy: The Virtuous Republic of Francesco Patrizi of Siena* (Cambridge, Mass.: Harvard University Press, 2023), p. 269.

6. Tom Ginsburg, Dan Rodriguez, and Barry Weingast, "Constitutional Monarchy as Equilibrium: Why Kings and Queens Survive in a World of Republics" (unpublished manuscript, September 2021), pp. 2–3. Note the difference in terminology, but the term "symbolic monarchy" is similar to constitutional monarchies that provide for rule by a symbolic monarch (in principle, the ideal of symbolic monarchy can be effective even without formal constitutional constraints, so I prefer the term "symbolic monarchy"). See also Dong Fangkui, "The Constitutional Monarchy and Modernization: Kang Youwei's Perspectives on 'Keeping the Emperor and Royal System in China,'" *Canadian Social Science* 10, no. 2 (2014): 1–8. Dong argues that constitutional monarchies developed in a more stable and rapid way compared with democratic republican countries in the twentieth century and he concludes that "the Constitutional Monarchy system should be acknowledged and promoted" (p. 8). He doesn't add "in China," but the implication is clear.

7. In China's imperial system, the monarch did not simply protect minority groups: Members of minority and outside groups such as Mongols and Manchus could even assume power as monarchs so long as they fulfilled the ritualistic ceremonies inherited from past dynasties.

8. These arguments draw on Ginsburg, Rodriguez, and Weingast, "Constitutional Monarchy as Equilibrium."

9. It is abstractly conceivable that a sage-king or queen is so perfect that he or she would not make bad decisions, in which case this argument would not be valid. For an imaginative account of a sage-queen ruling China in the year 2040, see Jean-Louis Roy, *Shanghai 2040* (Montreal: Libre Expression, 2021). Such a scenario for the future, regrettably, is unlikely. In history, it's hard to think of a single case of a ruler who never made a bad decision.

10. Hankins, *Political Meritocracy in Renaissance Italy*, p. 268.

11. Such informal norms for speeches by Chinese bureaucrats do not have any official justification. As far as I can tell, flat affect is meant to convey commitment to hard work and to the virtue of impartiality. In different settings—such as a dinner with friends, especially after a few drinks—the same person can be warm, funny, and a wonderful teller of stories that more clearly express personal likes and dislikes. The three-point norm is perhaps the middle ground between two extremes: The intended audience would find it too simplistic if the speaker made only one or two points and it might stop paying attention if there were too many points. The number four is usually avoided because it's an unlucky number in China—*si* 四, the number four, sounds similar to *si* 死, the word for death—and five points would be too many for most people to absorb, so three points seems about right. Sometimes bureaucrats embed many sub-points under the rubric of three points (I once counted thirty-seven sub-points in an eighty-five-minute speech by one of our faculty leaders; it was not a successful strategy to retain most people's attention).

12. Vivienne Shue argues that President Xi draws on the legacy of imperial ritual performance to resume "the positioning in the polity once presumed to be held by emperors." See Shue, "Regimes of Resonance: Cosmos, Empire, and Changing Technologies of CCP Rule," *Modern China*, January 11, 2022, p. 26 (https://journals.sagepub.com/doi/full/10.1177/00977004211068055). I first experienced this comparison in 2013 when a very well-connected businessman referred, almost in passing, to President Xi as "皇帝" (Emperor).

13. Edward Muir, *Civic Ritual in Renaissance Venice* (Princeton, N.J.: Princeton University Press, 1981), p. 186.

14. Ray Huang, *1587, a Year of No Significance: The Ming Dynasty in Decline* (New Haven, Conn.: Yale University Press, 1981), pp. 3, 76, 5.

15. Quoted in ibid., pp. 46–47.

16. President Xi himself said, "Happiness must be achieved through hard work" (official translation in http://www.xinhuanet.com/english/2021-08/11/c_1310121056.htm). The Chinese sentence reads "要幸福就要斗争," which can be translated more literally as "if you want happiness, you must struggle." The term "斗争" (struggle) has Marxist echoes of class struggle, but a more charitable interpretation is that President Xi meant something like "happiness comes from hard work and overcoming obstacles to serve the public." It's a fine ethos for bureaucrats, but there are other ways to be happy.

17. In December 2018, Meng Wanzhou, the chief financial officer of Huawei, was detained by Canadian authorities at the behest of the U.S. government, and two Canadians, Michael Kovrig and Michael Spavor, were detained in China shortly thereafter in apparent retaliation. Meng was held under house arrest at her luxury home in Vancouver and the "two Michaels" were held in appalling prison conditions.

During this period, Canadians in China (including me) worried that they might also be held as hostages if relations further deteriorated between the two governments. The three detainees were released in September 2021, so the argument that I needed to continue to serve as dean in order not to make it seem as though I had been purged for political reasons was no longer valid.

# INDEX

equality is good, 61–62; learning to navigate, 57–58; limiting dictatorship, 45–46; merits of, 59–64; need for free expression and critical viewpoints, 62–64; Shandong University, 46, 51

communism, 32; Confucianism and, 104–5; elections in, 100–101; higher, 99, 102; lower, 99. *See also* Marxism.

communitarianism, 11; from, to Confucianism, 11–13

*Confessions* (Augustine), 18

*Confessions* (Rousseau), 18, 27, 165n15

Confucianism (*Rujia*), 2, 3, 169n9; academic, 8; Chinese Communist Party and, 6–7; Chinese tradition, 118; from communitarianism to, 11–13; Confucian comeback, 4–11; debating, 88–90; difficulty promoting, 56; ethics, 9; founders of, 77; good life, 9; heritage, 162n14; history and philosophy of, 57; ideal best life, 46; Legalists and, 35; Mohists and, 35; promotion of, in China, 38, 49; revival in China, 9–11; revival of, 7; serving political community, 142–43; shame, 18; suppression in Qin Dynasty, 4; teaching, 49, 87–92; Western invention, 4

Confucius (*Kongzi*), 2, 90, 159; approach to life, 74; Confucius in the West, 4, 85; emojis of, 144; good life, 5; higher education, 85–87; privileges of descendants, 173n1; student Yan Hui, 93; symbolic monarchy in China, 150; teaching and drinking, 87–92; teaching and learning, 86; view of self, 4

Confucius Institutes, 7, 33

*Confucius Research* (*Kongzi Yanjiu*) (periodical), 8

Confucius temple, Kongzi statue at, 85

conservative, definition of, 161n5

Constitutional Monarchy system, 159, 184n6

coronavirus. *See* Covid

corruption, 30; buying of government posts (*mai guan*), 72; China, 65–67; Chinese public polls, 66

Covid, 153; campus examinations and, 180n8; deaths by, 68; halt of internationalization with, 57; helping colleagues during, 183n21; Johnson and, 145; Legalist-style coercion, 175n22; Li Wenliang and, 68, 113; lockdown of Shanghai, 182n16; mask-wearing and, 50; Omicron variant, 16; *shuji* protecting students and faculty from, 40–41; Wuhan and, 30, 142

CPPCC. *See* Chinese People's Political Consultative Conference (CPPCC)

*Crown, The* (show), 156

CSSCI (Chinese Social Science Citation Index), 132, 134, 148

Cui Shi, on salaries of public officials, 171n6

Cultural Revolution, 6, 7, 10; deemphasis on individuality, 22; experience of, 45; hair dyeing, 25

*Culture, History, and Philosophy* (*Wenshizhe*) (journal), 8, 162n12

culture of cuteness: term, 138. *See also* cuteness

cuteness: animal world, 141–42; culture of, 139–43; danger of, 143–44; depoliticized, 143; downside of culture of, 148; eccentricity and, 143–44; of elephants, 140–41; as human

Shanxi, 130

Shih, Victor, on Chinese political system, 62

Shue, Vivienne, legacy of imperial ritual performance, 185n12

*shuji. See* Party Secretary

Singapore, 12, 177n16; universities, 114

Slingerland, Edward, 74; on Confucius' drinking, 74

socialism, primary stage of, 101

*South China Morning Post* (newspaper), 113, 124

South Korea, 31

Soviet Union, 15

SSCI (Social Science Citation Index), 134, 148

Stalin, communism, 32

Standing Committee of the Politburo, 22–23, 46 59, 61, 63–64, 98, 184n2

Stanford University, Center for Advanced Study in the Behavioral Sciences, 26

Stasavage, David, on China's bureaucracy, 101

Sun, Anna, Chinese state's promotion of Confucianism, 10

symbolic leadership, lower levels of government, 153–59

symbolic monarchy: beauty of, 150–53; China, 150; separation of powers and, 151–52; symbolic and political powers, 152–53; term, 184n6

Taiwan, 8, 163n22, 176n5

thought work, political, 43

*tianxia* (all-under-heaven), 71

Tibetans, 10, 117

*Tongyi Zhanxian. See* United Front

Trump, Donald, 118; election of, 133–34; patriotic love of country, 153

Tsingdao (Qingdao) beer, 40

Tsinghua University, 2, 48, 50, 92, 166–67n6; Beijing students admittance to, 38; classroom freedom, 107; Department of Philosophy, 87, 132; faculty meetings at, 53; Mill's defense of free speech, 108; political meritocracy, 169n11, 178n25; political trouble at, 176n4; responsibility and cuteness, 146; School of Social Sciences, 8

Tu Weiming, as exponent of Confucianism in West, 7

Ukraine, Russia's invasion of, 14

"Union of Democratic Meritocrats", 110

United Front (*Tongyi Zhanxian*), work of, 34–36

United Kingdom: monarchy of, 150; separation of powers and, 151–52

United States, 8; China and, 15, 163n22, 163–64n23; Chinese students in, 15; demonization of China, 116–17; economics of China and, 117–19; love of country and Trump, 153; National Security Council, 163n20; separation of powers and, 151, 152; universities in, 116; U.S.-China relations, 163n20, 174n7

universities: dean, 46–59; developing world-class faculty, 181n13; entrance examinations (*gaokao*), 66, 91, 131, 180n7; female academics and, 181n11; Hong Kong, 181n10; internationalizing, 2–3; supervising doctoral students, 180n9; Western, 46, 107–8, 129, 132–33, 168n14, 181n15

University of Hawaii, Ames, 7
Uyghurs, 10, 14, 117

virtue, 60
Voice of America, 115

*Wall Street Journal* (newspaper), 60,
  110, 115, 124
Wang Pei, 18, 110, 112, 176n8
Wang Shaoguang, on Xi as first among
  equals, 23
Wang Xuedian, Shandong University, 8
Wanli (Emperor), 72, 154, 155
Warring States era, 52, 91, 162n14
Washington, George, 150
Weber, Max: on Confucianism, 8; on
  ethic of responsibility, 183n18
WeChat, 39, 41–42, 58, 168n3; use of
  emojis in, 144, 145
Weingast, Barry, on monarchs, 151
Western countries, anti-China turn in,
  136–37
West Point Military Academy, 90,
  174n7
white hair, 164n5; Mencius on, 21; sign
  of, 22
white liquor (*bai jiu*), 70, 75, 80, 84;
  Lanling, 92
"Wolf Warrior" rhetoric, 138

World Expo, Shanghai, 109
World Trade Organization, 163n19
Wuhan: Covid, 16, 30, 142; debacle of, 72

Xenophon's *Cyropaedia*, 153
Xinjiang, 30
*Xuanchuanbu. See* Publicity
  Department
Xunzi: education and ritual, 81; follower of Confucius, 4; as a founder
  of Confucianism, 77; on hegemon
  (*ba*), 79; on humane king (*wang*),
  78–79, 80, 172n5; informal rituals
  of ruler, 79–80; law and ritual, 80;
  on military power, 79; political
  thought, 91, 92; ritual participation,
  77–78; rituals, 80, 172n6; student
  Han Feizi, 93

Yang Dali, Shandong University hire,
  161n3
Yan Xuetong, realist thinker, 164n23
Yongzhen (Emperor), 170n18
Yuan Guiren, on Marxist ideology,
  106
Yunnan Province, elephants in, 140–41

Zhang Li, 42–43
Zuo Zhuan, 33